PARENTS DIAGNOSE
AND
CORRECT READING PROBLEMS

For Parents of Children with
Reading Disabilities

PARENTS DIAGNOSE AND CORRECT READING PROBLEMS

For Parents of Children with Reading Disabilities

By

HAROLD D. LOVE, Ed.D.
State College of Arkansas
Conway, Arkansas

CHARLES C THOMAS • PUBLISHER
Springfield • *Illinois* • *U.S.A.*

Published and Distributed Throughout the World by
CHARLES C THOMAS • PUBLISHER
BANNERSTONE HOUSE
301-327 East Lawrence Avenue, Springfield, Illinois, U.S.A.

NATCHEZ PLANTATION HOUSE
735 North Atlantic Boulevard, Fort Lauderdale, Florida, U.S.A.

This book is protected by copyright. No part of it may be reproduced in any manner without written permission from the publisher.

© *1970, by* **CHARLES C THOMAS • PUBLISHER**
Library of Congress Catalog Card Number: 70-122204

With **THOMAS BOOKS** *careful attention is given to all details of manufacturing and design. It is the Publisher's desire to present books that are satisfactory as to their physical qualities and artistic possibilities and appropriate for their particular use.* **THOMAS BOOKS** *will be true to those laws of quality that assure a good name and good will.*

Printed in the United States of America
T-1

To
CARLTON MOORE,
MARILYN TAGGART
and
WENDY LOVE

PREFACE

THIS book was written beause the author firmly believes that parents can diagnose and correct their children's reading problems. Children who get into difficulty with reading need immediate help, and must have their reading problems diagnosed and corrected if they are to gain the reading ability needed to function in life today. Children spend approximately 80 per cent of their time at home. They are with their mothers and fathers more than with any other people in their environment. It appears logical then that parents know their children very well and that with basic knowledge concerning diagnosis and corrective techniques they can do a valuable job supplementing the school's role in evaluating reading ability and correcting deficiencies.

During my college days, while majoring in remedial reading and working in the college reading clinic, I came into contact with many children having reading difficulties and also with the parents of these children. It was my contention then that parents could help their children. I told the parents of my belief and conducted a follow-through study to determine the results. With basic help in reading techniques, parents were invariably successful in helping their children. Later as a reading teacher I observed the same truism. I also observed that most parents are very much interested in the welfare of their children and realize that without the most important tool of all—reading—the child is denied many of the important things in his life. For these and many other reasons, I have written this book for parents.

I wish to thank Katty Crownover and Linda Taylor for their diligent work in typing the manuscript. Special thanks are extended to Florine and Cindy Bell who read and criticized the manuscript, to Betty Young and Mary Robinson for many helpful editorial suggestions, and to Jerry Poole and Jan Guthrie who did the illustrations. Lastly, I wish to express my deep gratitude to Sue M. Love for her extensive help in all phases of the preparation of the manuscript.

HDL

CONTENTS

	Page
Preface	vii

Chapter
1. WHAT PARENTS SHOULD KNOW 3
2. INFORMAL READING INVENTORY FOR PARENTS 14
3. READING READINESS AND READINESS TESTS 33
4. READING AND CHILD DEVELOPMENT 40
5. CAUSES OF READING PROBLEMS 48
6. WORD RECOGNITION AND COMPREHENSION 55
7. YOUR CHILD'S INTEREST AND TASTE IN READING 71
8. STUDY SKILLS 77
9. CHILDREN WITH LEARNING DISABILITIES 85
10. PARENTS HELP THE GIFTED 93
11. ORAL AND SILENT READING 100

Index 107

PARENTS DIAGNOSE AND CORRECT READING PROBLEMS

For Parents of Children with Reading Disabilities

Chapter 1

WHAT PARENTS SHOULD KNOW

THERE has been some controversy but little research concerning the parents' role in helping their children when they develop a reading problem. Since reading is the most important aspect of the child's academic life, it is necessary that he have all the encouragement and assistance he needs to help him develop and perfect the ability to read well.

Parents often ask each other, Why can't the school teach my child to read well? The best answer to this question is that schools in America do an excellent job where the teaching of reading is concerned but that this extremely difficult and abstract task is harder for some children to master than for others. Why? There are at least two hundred known reasons why a child lags behind his classmates in reading. Many of these reasons will be discussed later in the book.

DEFINITION OF A READING PROBLEM

When a child's performance lags behind his ability by one or more years in word recognition, word attack skills, comprehension, or listening skills, he is said to have a reading problem. Naturally some children have a more acute problem than others. Also, a child may lag behind the other children in one or all of the skills mentioned—word recognition, word attack, comprehension, and listening.

Word recognition is the ability to recognize the whole word immediately without thinking of the beginning, middle, or ending sounds. *Word attack* skill is the ability to distinguish properly the beginning, middle, and ending of a word. Naturally, *comprehension* is the amount of information retained by the child from the passage read. At this point, parents should be informed that even the fast reader has a comprehension problem if his comprehension falls below 75 per cent.

The fourth facet of reading is *listening*. The child should be able to listen to passages read aloud to him and answer at least 75 per cent of the questions covering the passages. Generally, a child who has poor listening skills also has poor word recognition skills.

PARENTS TEACH

For some obscure reason parents have been told for many years that they cannot do an adequate job in diagnosing and correcting the reading problems of their children. Generally, the reason given has been that parents become too emotionally involved in the process to do a good job. Historically, parents have been encouraged to help their children in math. The so-called new math had parents throughout the country taking courses in order that they could help their children. Parents are encouraged to help in other school areas such as English, history, spelling, social studies, and geography, but not in reading. Parents have been told to keep hands off when it comes to the most important academic tool in life. Why? Very little research has been conducted to determine the effectiveness with which parents can diagnose and correct the reading difficulties of their children. This book is based upon the supposition that most parents can do an excellent job in helping their child master reading if a few basic steps are followed and some foundation information is learned.

Within one family there may be children reading at various stages, and not all of them will always be functioning at their own grade level. As a matter of fact, in any elementary class, reading achievement levels can vary as much as twelve grades. For example, at the beginning of the second grade the variance in reading can range from readiness to fourth-grade level. Each succeeding year increases the spread.

Under such circumstances, some informal way of evaluating reading ability, put into the hands of interested parents, can be a valuable guide for them. In diagnosing reading ability, parents can use the regular classroom materials. In fact, informal tests using regular classroom materials are the best way to determine where the child is presently reading and how to improve his reading ability. In the next chapter, an informal reading inventory for parents will be discussed in detail.

Parents often hear about new methods for teaching reading and about the advantages of one method over another. All of the methods known to man have been used in American classrooms for years with good and poor results. All the methods for teaching reading have their strengths and weaknesses.

The most important element in teaching reading is the teacher, not the method. A good teacher uses many methods, adding her own improvements to classroom instruction as her years of experience accumulate.

It is amazing to this author how people having little experience with children and no experience in teaching can sit back and say that one method or one teacher is superior or inferior to another. Very often a parent will say, "My child is not getting enough phonics." Actually, that parent does not know whether his child is or is not getting instruction in phonics (the teaching of letters and combinations of letters that create certain sounds) in the approach to reading. One thing is for certain, though: if the teacher is using the basal reading series and following the teacher's manual, then the child is being adequately exposed to phonics.

WHERE TO START

Parents ask, What can I do to improve my child's reading ability and interests? There are many things parents can do. They may contribute richly even before the child goes to school by helping him engage in language activities. Contrary to popular belief, learning to read begins at birth and continues throughout the life of the individual. The parents should answer the child's questions as fully and meaningfully as possible. They should talk to him, tell him stories, read to him, and encourage him to talk. In addition, he should be provided with books and magazines at home. There are many good books and magazines today that are printed specifically for the young child. There are also picture cards and games, alphabet books, picture and story books, and books related to the child's individual interests. Local librarians are happy to be of assistance in finding books for a child on his reading level.

Tours of local stores, factories, plants, parks, and zoos as well as longer scenic vacation trips can be very educational and can add to the child's reading skills. Along the way the parents should engage the child in conversation, call his attention to interesting sights, read signs and advertisements, and talk about them.

This same pattern of family activity can be carried out through college. The child should always know that his comments, reports, and questions are considered important and that no matter is too small or too silly to be discussed if he has a question or comment on it.

Before he is ready for formal reading, the child must be able to speak and express himself well enough for others to understand him. The greater a child's listening and speaking abilities prior to entering school, the greater his readiness to do first-grade work. Therefore, the more the child is encouraged to participate in conversation, the better prepared he will be for the experiences of the formal reading program of the school and, hence, the more success he will experience. Rushing children into the formal reading readiness program before they are ready is one of the chief causes of reading problems.

In the next chapter you will find an informal reading inventory similar to one used by many classroom teachers for assessing the reading level of each child in the classroom. The teacher or parent may give the test to a group of children or to individuals, depending on the class and the reason for administering the test. Informal reading inventories give a much more valid indication of the individual's reading ability than standardized tests because no norms have been established. The pupil is not compared with the majority or with another child in his own classroom; instead his skills are assessed against perfection and his results are compared with the results of his own earlier performances.

VALUABLE TIPS

The numerical grades such as A, B, C, D, and F awarded in most schools for performance in reading do not always indicate how well a child is reading. Grades vary from teacher to teacher and often lose all meaning when applied to actual performance. For example, a teacher may give only A, B, or C grades. This, of course, is not a bad situation, but the child who receives a C in reading may not be able to read at all. With some stricter teachers, a C grade may indicate that the child is reading above average. In some cases a teacher may award the grade of F to a mentally retarded child who is reading at his expected level but not at the level of grade placement. It should be noted at this point that not all children who read below grade placement have a reading problem. A child has a reading difficulty only **if he is reading one year below his mental ability level.** Therefore, a bright nine-year-old who is reading at the fourth-grade level could have a reading problem. According to his mental ability, he possibly should be reading at the sixth-grade level although he is in the fourth grade.

The above statements are true; therefore the informal reading inventory is an even more valuable tool for the parent to use to find out how well his child actually is reading. Naturally, it will benefit the child and the parent if the child's intellectual ability is also known. Very often, though, parents do not have access to this information. However, this does not mean that the parent cannot still utilize the informal reading inventory to determine his child's reading ability and help him develop better skills and habits.

A WARNING

One very important thing should be mentioned at this time. Once you discover that your child has a reading problem, do not expect it to be corrected overnight. Let us take a sixth-grader, for example, who is reading at the third-grade level. It has taken twelve years for this child to develop a reading deficiency that is obvious to his parents and teacher. How can one expect this problem to be conquered in a week or even a month?

Corrective reading takes time; therefore, remedial and preventive measures should be started as early as possible. This is another reason why parents should evaluate their children with an informal reading inventory.

AVOIDING CRITICISM

Parents are sensitive creatures where their children are concerned, torn between the desire to help and an impatience to see progress, while the growing child is dependent on the love and approval of the adults in his home. Every time it is necessary for one of the adult family members to correct the child's pronunciation of a word, supply a word in his reading that he has difficulty remembering, or even correct his spelling, there is implied criticism. An unintended implication on the part of the parent may cause the child to experience unduly strong fear—fear that he will lose parental love and approval. For this reason, the parent must be patient and not imply or overtly impart criticism. The teaching of reading requires patience, knowledge, and stated love as well as genuine affection.

CORRECTIVE INSTRUCTION

It can be said that the job of the corrective teacher is to bring about in the area of reading what might have been. The word *teacher* in the previous sentence does not imply a person who is professionally trained to be a classroom teacher. The word does imply anyone who takes the time and has the knowledge to help a child with reading retardation that can be eliminated without going to special clinics. Therefore, if the correction can be effected by parents using sound principles and procedures for developmental work, this should be done. If this can be done, it must be admitted that the problem could probably have been avoided in the first place.

The starting point for corrective instruction by parents must be not only identification of where the child presently is reading, but identification of the situations that led to the growth of the problem. For example, we must find out what basic principles of learning were ignored when instruction was first given. What obstacles were allowed to stand in the child's path? For example, does he have a hearing problem or a vision problem? Does he have a personality maladjustment? Only in this way can the best efforts of the child, the parents, and his teachers be utilized to help him overcome his reading lag. The next chapter will deal with finding the child's level of reading and another chapter will deal with the causes of the child's reading problem.

DYSLEXIA

Twenty years ago the word *dyslexia* was seldom a part of parents' speaking and reading vocabulary. Today it is very much a part of the lives of many parents. Dyslexia can adequately be described as *symbol blindness*. A small percentage of children suffering from reading disabilities have dyslexia or symbol blindness. These are the children who are reading two-and-a-half to three years below grade placement but still are intellectually normal. It must be pointed out that for these children, who probably suffer from minimal brain damage, professional help is needed along with parental help, love, and tolerance. The parent cannot alone correct the reading problem of the child who suffers from dyslexia. But it must be pointed out that the parent can be of vital help in overcoming the reading problems of the dyslexic child. It should also be pointed out to parents that although the child suffering from dyslexia can be helped, it is a long, drawn-out process, often taking from four to six years or even longer. The child suffering from dyslexia can be diagnosed fairly early in his reading career. This is the child who is not ready for the first grade and is not ready to begin reading when the other first-graders begin. Generally, at the end of the first grade this child cannot pronounce 25 per cent of the words in the primer and can only pronounce about 10 per cent of the words in the first-grade basal reader. This is the time that the parent can become aware that his child has a serious reading problem. If the parent has access to the basal reader, it is very easy for him to determine whether his child can pronounce 10 per cent of the words.

THE READING PROCESS

Reading is the meat and potatoes of the entire curriculum. In every subject the pupils' learning activities involve reading. In the content areas such as history, social studies, and geography, the student uses textbooks, reference books, and library reading. Even in handwriting and art, in the early elementary grades, children must read from printed guides and manuals. In the elementary grades the teacher writes assignments and instructions on the chalkboard to be read by the children. Reading is truly the basic tool of learning in all subjects.

As stated earlier in this chapter, reading is a very complex activity. It involves many skills: the ability to focus the eyes on the printed page, to move them from side to side and follow the lines of print, to hear the differences in words that resemble each other, to figure out new words, to select the main points in a paragraph; it is also the ability to adjust one's rate of speed and to put a meaningful inflection in one's voice.

As the student reads, he must also think and follow the line of thought the author has expressed, and he must be able to recall what has been printed. Then he must evaluate the information and draw conclusions. Word calling is not reading, although many people confuse the two. Without comprehension, word calling is almost useless.

A person who lives in our world and cannot read is living almost in darkness. Not a day goes by that he does not need to read. If he goes to the grocery store, he needs to read. If he goes to a movie, he must read. If he goes downtown, he reads. If he walks across the street, he reads, and certainly to go to the polls and vote he must be able to read. Reading is as much a form of communication as are speaking, listening, and writing. It is a way of expressing and exchanging ideas. When we write a letter we are communicating. When we receive a letter we are communicating. In each case we must be able to read.

STAGES IN READING

It takes years for a child to master the skills involved in reading. As stated earlier in this chapter, reading actually begins at birth and evolves until the day we die. The first stage in formal reading is the development of initial reading readiness. The young child must have many, many experiences to acquire a large enough vocabularly to be ready to read.

During the first stage, the child acquires a sizable vocabulary and develops auditory discrimination so that he hears the sound in words correctly. He must also speak the words precisely and learn to enunciate properly.

The second stage of reading sees the child getting his first instruction through the use of chalkboards, charts, labels, and teacher-prepared materials. It must be pointed out that the parents should help in every stage of reading development. This is certainly a job not just for the teacher but for the entire family. As the child learns to start at the left-hand side of the page and read from left to right, he acquires a stock of words he knows at sight. He now can give meaning to these words in many situations. At the same time he knows that he must read from top to bottom.

Once the child has gone through the second stage of reading, he moves on to the third, which is mastering the basic reading skills. He begins to increase his sight vocabulary, and he learns ways of figuring out new words. At this time, if he is adequately progressing, he also comprehends approximately 90 per cent of what he reads.

During the fourth stage, the child increases his efficiency at a very rapid pace. He now can figure out multisyllable words.

During the fifth stage, the child is at the fifth- and sixth-grade level. He has refined his reading to a great extent, and uses it as a mode of enjoyment and a tool in learning.

During the sixth stage of reading, the child should have refined this skill to the point where he can skim, read casually, or study carefully. He should be able to use effectively dictionaries and encyclopedias, his oral and silent reading is now smooth, and he can competently figure out almost all words.

READINESS STAGE

At the readiness stage in reading there should be a great deal of listening on the part of the child. The teacher or parent will

Chapter 2

INFORMAL READING INVENTORY FOR PARENTS

How can I tell if my child is reading at his grade level? Many parents ask this question throughout the child's entire school life. They find that the numerical grades of A, B, C, etc., do not always indicate the child's reading level; therefore, many of them would like to be able to "check" their child themselves.

An informal reading inventory has many uses, but for the parent, it serves as a guide in finding the child's reading level in relation to his grade placement. It also shows where the child is having difficulty in his reading, and where his strongest areas are.

There are five different reading levels in which a child may be placed: A, B, C, D, and F.

The A reading level is the highest one; at this level the child can read and get the full meaning from what he has read. He works on his own and does the work almost perfectly. He shows no signs of difficulty such as using his finger to follow the printed lines while reading, moving his lips as he reads, reading in a voice so soft that he cannot be heard, or being tense during the reading. He should be able to read the material orally, missing only one or two words. When checking for comprehension, or how much he can remember from what he has read, he should be able to answer nine out of ten questions, or 90 per cent. He should also be able to find *context clues,* which tell him if the material is funny or critical, and which help him to understand the author's message.

The B reading level is the lowest level at which the child can profit from instruction. He is a good reader who does not show any signs of difficulty, and he should be able to read in an easy, flowing manner. He should be able to read faster silently than orally. He is expected to recognize 90 per cent of the words and should be able to understand about 90 per cent of the material he has read.

The C reading level is the point at which the child becomes confused and shows signs of tension and frustration. He often does not understand the words, and he may become very confused if the sentence is long. The signs of frustration are easy for parents to recognize. The child may read in a high-pitched voice or a single tone of voice, frown, squint, wriggle in his chair, yawn, cough, use his finger as a pointer in reading, move his lips as he reads to himself, substitute words, omit words, bite his fingernails, or develop other nervous mannerisms. He will probably recognize less than 75 per cent of the words and will be able to understand only half of what he reads. This child is definitely uncomfortable at this reading level.

The D level is the lowest level at which the child can understand material that is read to him. The parent must first find out if the child actually understands what he hears. This is done by asking the child questions after he has listened to the material. He should be able to answer the questions using almost exactly the same words that were in the printed passage. The child should understand 90 per cent of what he hears.

The F reading level is indicated when the child pronounces correctly less than 50 per cent of the words three years below his grade placement and has a listening comprehension of less than 50 per cent. Very often the child who falls into the F level can be classified as dyslexic. This, of course, is true only if the child has average intelligence. The first two chapters of this book mention average intelligence several times. Parents should be advised that only 3 per cent of the school-age population is classified as mentally retarded.

The informal reading inventory for parents determines three areas of proficiency: word recognition, oral and silent comprehension, and listening. To determine the child's reading ability, the parent must administer the individual inventory to the pupil at successively higher levels until the child reaches the point at which he can no longer read adequately.

INSTRUCTIONS FOR ADMINISTERING THE INVENTORY

The parents should read the material carefully so as to be familiar with the content and to know how to score the results. The inventory will generally come from the basal reading series in which the child is presently placed in school. Naturally, it will be advisable for the parent to get the basal reader for his child. For example, if the child is reading at the fourth-grade level, he may need the basal readers from the third, fourth, and fifth grades. However, a parent may use the guidelines in this chapter without utilizing his child's basal reader.

On the word recognition list, notice that there is a blank beside each word under the heading "Answer." Put a check (√) in the "Answer" blank if the child does not respond correctly and immediately.

The score is based on percentages and there will be twenty-five words at each level; therefore, each word will count 4 per cent. If a child misses two words at his reading level, he will score 92 per cent.

If the child is in September or October of the third grade, the parents should use the second-grade word list. If the child is in November or December of the third grade, the parents should use the third-grade list, etc.

Parents can use a slotted sheet of paper to expose the words, always remembering to expose only one word at a time. Figure 1 shows the slotted paper and how it is used.

Parents should start with the comprehension test one grade lower than the child's grade placement. The parents should read from a basal reader and ask the child ten questions concerning each paragraph; each question would be worth 10 per cent. The parents also can utilize the words in the lists at each level and make up a story using several of them. For example, they might pick ten words from the third-grade list and use them in a story, relating it to the child, then ask him ten ques-

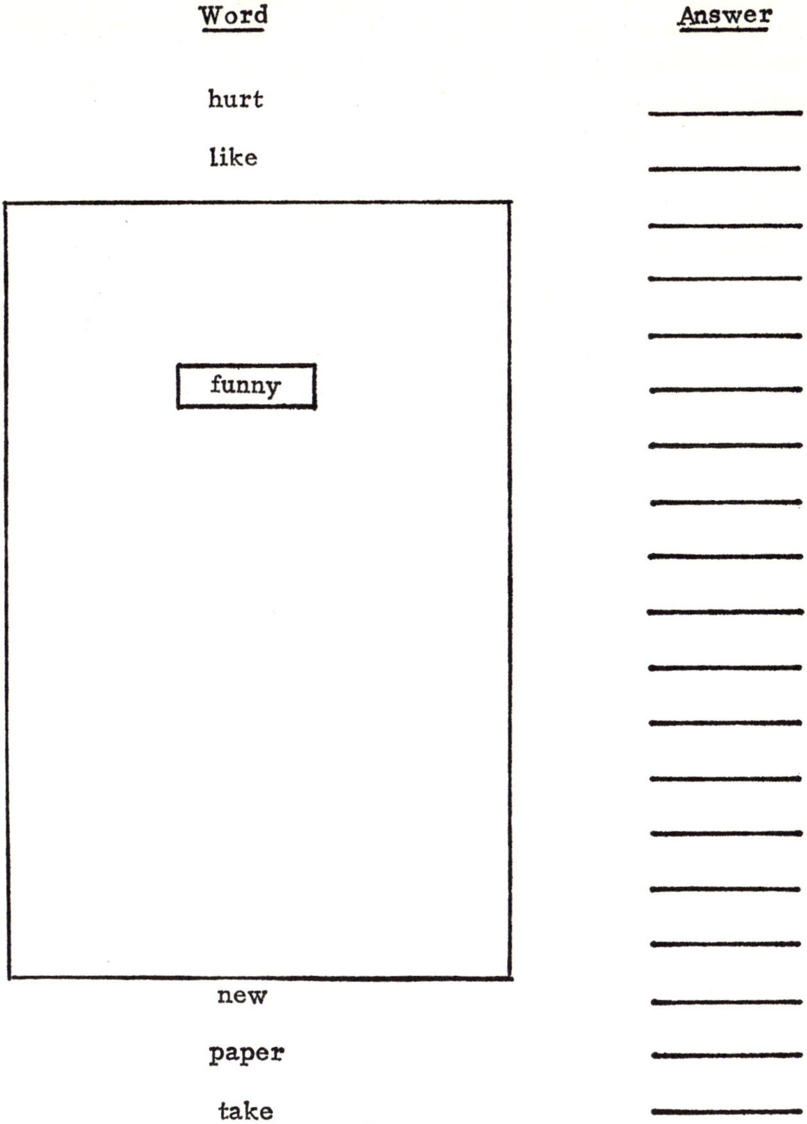

Word	Answer
hurt	_____
like	_____

funny

new	_____
paper	_____
take	_____

FIGURE 1

tions concerning the paragraph that has been read to him.

The objective is to determine the frustration level of the child. If he is reading adequately at his grade placement, then of course no provisions should be made for corrective reading.

Also, parents should know that if the child can pronounce

75 per cent of the words correctly at his grade placement, he has no serious reading problem. Ninety per cent would be much better, of course, but 75 per cent indicates a passing performance at his grade placement.

THE INVENTORY

On the following pages, parents will find several word lists representing each grade level from pre-primer through sixth grade. Utilizing a sheet of paper with a slot in it as indicated in Figure 1, the parents should cover each word with the slot and slide the paper down the word list, exposing one word at a time. Each word represents four percentage points. For example, if a child misses three words, he will score 88 per cent. When the parents reach the grade level where the child scores 75 per cent or less, they know that this is his frustration level.

The parents should then make up a short story, typing it or printing it on a sheet of 8½ x 11 white typing paper. The story should contain three-fourths of the words at one of the levels. In other words, if the child is being tested at the third-grade level, 75 per cent of the words at that level should be included in a short paragraph. The child should then read that story aloud to the parents. The good reader will breeze through the story with very few errors.

The parents should then make up a little story that is rich in facts. This story is read aloud by the parents to the child, after which the parents ask ten questions concerning the story. The child should score above 90 per cent to be considered excellent. If he scores below 75 per cent on comprehension, he is considered deficient in listening skills.

WORD RECOGNITION TEST
Pre-primer Level

Word	Answer
for	_____
to	_____
me	_____
go	_____
up	_____
we	_____
run	_____
it	_____
get	_____
will	_____
father	_____
the	_____
boy	_____
not	_____
ball	_____
you	_____
is	_____
mother	_____
and	_____
in	_____
a	_____
I	_____
here	_____
can	_____
out	_____

WORD RECOGNITION TEST
Primer Level

Word	Answer
she	_____
good	_____
her	_____
no	_____
on	_____
one	_____
put	_____
his	_____
at	_____
do	_____
this	_____
yes	_____
he	_____
book	_____
fire	_____
eat	_____
girl	_____
man	_____
may	_____
like	_____
are	_____
we	_____
new	_____
my	_____
take	_____

Informal Reading Inventory for Parents

WORD RECOGNITION TEST
First-Reader Level

Word	Answer
old	_____
took	_____
last	_____
give	_____
many	_____
happy	_____
know	_____
again	_____
when	_____
dog	_____
his	_____
over	_____
face	_____
was	_____
water	_____
stay	_____
let	_____
as	_____
but	_____
of	_____
old	_____
time	_____
had	_____
him	_____
while	_____

WORD RECOGNITION TEST
Second-Grade Level

Word	Answer
don't	_____
much	_____
air	_____
knew	_____
noise	_____
second	_____
bark	_____
tie	_____
hurry	_____
these	_____
visit	_____
glass	_____
always	_____
oh	_____
every	_____
same	_____
fix	_____
real	_____
dress	_____
farm	_____
hard	_____
side	_____
bad	_____
better	_____
hill	_____

WORD RECOGNITION TEST
Third-Grade Level

Word	Answer
saved	_____
worry	_____
teach	_____
pause	_____
deep	_____
born	_____
heard	_____
shine	_____
led	_____
pencil	_____
mail	_____
team	_____
stamp	_____
cheer	_____
above	_____
chair	_____
blast	_____
score	_____
whole	_____
apples	_____
pie	_____
east	_____
win	_____
lap	_____
price	_____

WORD RECOGNITION TEST
Fourth-Grade Level

Word	Answer
locked	_____
life	_____
gentle	_____
steal	_____
energy	_____
tone	_____
least	_____
sails	_____
notice	_____
shadow	_____
gown	_____
match	_____
ruin	_____
hero	_____
mine	_____
ocean	_____
mind	_____
between	_____
tower	_____
crew	_____
begun	_____
reward	_____
tramp	_____
worth	_____
rescue	_____

Informal Reading Inventory for Parents 25

WORD RECOGNITION TEST
Fifth-Grade Level

Word	*Answer*
attempt	_____
vicious	_____
twine	_____
character	_____
shallow	_____
habit	_____
manners	_____
season	_____
lime	_____
panic	_____
style	_____
gulf	_____
seize	_____
terror	_____
sob	_____
rather	_____
worship	_____
slope	_____
crawl	_____
spider	_____
shape	_____
jungle	_____
section	_____
pound	_____
plenty	_____

WORD RECOGNITION TEST
Sixth-Grade Level

Word	Answer
Permit	_____
neglect	_____
frequently	_____
enormous	_____
pleasure	_____
moisture	_____
novel	_____
physical	_____
social	_____
afford	_____
fierce	_____
irate	_____
chapter	_____
original	_____
swarm	_____
routine	_____
mechanics	_____
diamond	_____
casual	_____
courage	_____
dare	_____
abandon	_____
sketches	_____
model	_____
prospect	_____

ORAL READING AND SILENT COMPREHENSION

As stated previously in the chapter, the child should read a passage aloud to determine his frustration level for reading aloud. The parents can utilize the basal reading series that their child is presently reading in school. However, they also may employ the author's oral and silent comprehension series, examples of which are given on the next few pages.

DIRECTIONS

The child should read aloud the passage that is one year lower than his present grade placement. In case he cannot read this level adequately, his parents should allow him to go down to the point where he can read smoothly. He should then progress upward. The frustration level is reached in oral reading when the child is missing 25 per cent of the words.

After the oral frustration level has been reached, the child is allowed to read the same passages silently. The parents then ask the questions listed below each passage. The child should never miss more than one question. When he misses 25 per cent of the questions, his frustration level for comprehension has been reached.

ORAL READING AND SILENT COMPREHENSION TEST

Pre-primer Level

"Mother!" said Betty.
"A boy ran after the ball.
His name is John.
John has a little sister.
Her name is Mary."

1. To whom is Betty speaking?
2. What did the boy run after?
3. Who ran after the ball?
4. Who is Mary's brother?
5. Who is John's sister?

Primer Level

Betty said one day,
"Mother and I go to town.
We like to buy new things.
She gets me toys.
She gets me books,
I like to play with them."

1. Where is Betty going?
2. What are they going to do in town?
3. What does Betty get new?
4. What does Betty do with her new toys?
5. Who is going with Betty?

First-Reader Level

One day Johnny was going to play. He stopped to look at the rabbits. One jumped out of his box. He jumped into the wagon. Johnny took his wagon. He went to play.

1. Who stopped to look at the rabbits?
2. Where was he going when he stopped to see them?
3. How many rabbits jumped out of the box?
4. What did the rabbit jump into?
5. What did Johnny do after the rabbit jumped into the wagon?

Second-Reader Level

There was one thing Billy Brown liked very much. He liked to play that he was a fireman. He always watched when a fire truck went by.

He had watched firemen use a big fire hose to put out the fire.

He had learned how to call a fireman if he saw a fire and what to say.

1. What was the boy's name in our story?
2. What did Billy like to play that he was?
3. What did he always watch go by?
4. What did Billy watch the firemen use?
5. What two things did Billy learn to do?

Third-Reader Level

We had a very bad fire after the circus was over. It spread rapidly from building to building. Finally, the building with the horses in it began to burn. There were twenty horses in it.

Animals, especially horses, are very quick to sense danger. Those twenty horses were out of the barn before anyone even knew it was on fire. They got out in a very orderly way.

They all got out through the door. Not one was hurt or tried to run away.

1. What happened after the circus was over?
2. How did the fire spread?
3. What are horses very quick to sense?
4. How many horses were there?
5. How did the horses get out of the building?
6. How many horses were hurt?
7. How many horses ran away?

Fourth-Reader Level

In the early morning sunlight, John Smith gazed with pleasure at the buckets of honey in front of him. There was one gallon in one bucket and another gallon in a bucket in the canoe.

"Won't the men at camp be surprised when they see these two gallons of fresh honey?" he thought to himself.

He was about to pick up the bucket when he heard a strange noise behind him. When he turned quickly around, he faced a huge, black, unfriendly bear standing between him and the canoe.

1. Did this story take place in the morning or afternoon?
2. What was John doing?
3. How many pails of honey did he have?
4. What is a gallon?
5. What was making the strange noise that John heard?
6. What color was the animal?
7. How was John getting back to camp?
8. Was the bear friendly?

Fifth-Reader Level

Recently, six men decided to explore the moon. They took their material and equipment with them and began working in two's. With space suits on to protect them from the extreme heat, they shoveled great mounds of dirt from the spot where they believed gold to be buried. One man used a sifter made of loosely bound pieces of wire and held it over the cooking pan while the other shoveled dirt into the sifter. When the pan was full, the men carried it to the water container and lowered it into the water. Then with sticks they stirred the moon dirt until most of it flowed over the top of the pan and settled in the bottom of the container. What was left they placed in the sun to dry. When it had dried, black gold lay shining in the bottom of the pan, sometimes in pieces about the size of a pecan but more often in the form of dust.

1. How many men worked in a group?
2. Was it cold or hot where they landed on the moon?
3. How do we know that they had to do a lot of shoveling?
4. How many men went on the moon trip?
5. What was the sifter made of?

6. What did the men use to stir the dirt?
7. What did the men do when the pan was full?
8. What did they find in the moon dirt?
9. How large were some of the pieces of black gold?
10. In what form was the gold usually found?

Sixth-Reader Level

Shore Patrol officers are always alert. Their enemies are high winds, storms, and foul weather. Shore Patrol stations are scattered all along the coast of the United States. Their job is to save lives and property from storms. They must keep navigation routes patrolled for icebergs or other hazardous conditions. They must also keep the cities along the shoreline posted on weather conditions and notify the people to evacuate in case of a severe storm. The work of these men saves thousands of lives each year and millions of dollars of property.

1. Who must always be alert?
2. Name three enemies of the Shore Patrol.
3. What does "scattered all along the coast" mean?
4. Name two duties of the Shore Patrol officers.
5. What must the Shore Patrol officers look for on navigation routes?
6. What is a navigation route?
7. What does *evacuate* mean?
8. How many lives are saved by the Shore Patrol each year?
9. What kind of property do they save?
10. What is the job of each patrolman?

AFTER THE INVENTORY IS GIVEN

The parents should remember that the object is to go as high as the child can read until the frustration level has been reached. A fourth-grade child may find that the second grade is his frustration level. Corrective reading for this child then would begin at the first-grade level. Corrective reading should always begin at a level one year lower than the frustration level if the child has a reading problem. In the beginning stages of corrective reading the child should be able to do the work as easily as cutting through warm butter. This gives him confidence and the desire to move ahead.

In the informal reading inventory, the word recognition section is more important than the oral reading and silent comprehension section. It is important, however, that the child read aloud to the parents so that they can observe any nervous mannerisms that will indicate that he is uncomfortable at that reading level.

For most children, if word recognition is sufficiently high, comprehension and listening skills will also be high.

In some cases, the child will have a sufficient word attack but will be deficient in comprehension. In this case, the corrective reading should be concentrated in the area of comprehension, with word recognition drill being secondary. Seldom, though, will the child be high in comprehension and low in word recognition.

Parents may encounter children who are high in comprehension but who show signs of frustration when reading aloud. The practice in a case like this should be word recognition, but the parents also should try to determine if the audience has anything to do with the child being nervous while reading aloud. Many children become nervous just because they have been asked to read aloud. These same children may be able to read very well silently. This certainly should be determined by the parents before corrective instruction is administered.

As stated previously, the informal reading inventory is a valuable tool to compare the child against himself. For example, if the child is tested by the parents in September, his record should be kept; he should be tested again in November and possibly in March, and then in May. After each testing session, the parents should compare his progress and determine the degree of progress. Only by keeping the old inventories can the parents compare the new one and find out exactly how the child is doing.

Chapter 3

READING READINESS AND READINESS TESTS

READING troubles initially appear in the first few weeks of the first grade. The child's reading proficiency in these few weeks determines to a large extent his success or failure in reading. Because a child has had little formal reading instruction before the first grade, this is where his reading difficulties begin and where he meets frustration in learning to read symbols. It is also in the first grade that the first emotional problems manifest themselves in relation to reading. If the reading readiness program is a good one, most reading difficulties can be avoided. A good reading readiness program must be defined, because not only is it a difficult program to carry out, but in addition many people do not understand it thoroughly. There are children who must stay in a reading readiness program for as long as two years before they are actually ready for the first instruction in reading. These children are mentally retarded and have IQs between 50 and 75. There are other children who have IQs between 75 and 90 who need a full year of reading readiness before they are ready for the reading process. Fifty per cent of the children in the elementary school system need about two months of reading readiness before they are ready for the reading process. About 10 per cent of the children who enter first grade are ready to read the first day of the school session. And about 5 per cent of the children entering first grade can read before the first day of school.

As you can see, a reading readiness program is not an easy one to administer or teach; each child is different and his differences must be met if he is to be ready to read at the proper time.

BACKGROUND ABILITIES

A great deal of research has been done in relation to the environments of children who learn to read quickly as compared with the environments of children who have a great deal of trouble. It is evident that differences in success in reading depend upon many prereading abilities that a child acquires through the home, nursery schools, and kindergartens. A very bright child could still be deficient in some of these abilities and not be ready to learn to read in the first grade.

The first assumption for determining the child's readiness to read is that he has average intelligence. We can assume that if the child has an IQ of 90 or above, he has average intelligence and should be ready to read, as long as he does not have too many deficiencies in his background, at about the age of six and a half. The child who ranks at the low end of the average scale of intelligence and has a birthday falling very close to September 1 will not be as ready to read as the child who has a birthday in March or April. There is an old saying that March and April babies do well in school. This assumes, of course, that they have average or above-average intelligence. They do better in school because they are generally six and a half years old before they begin school; therefore, they have several months of practice that the other children do not have.

Children must be able to distinguish among word elements as they pertain to visual and auditory discrimination. In other words, to be ready for reading the child should be able to recognize that words have different shapes and that these shapes are meaningful; he also should know there are different sounds to words and be able to recognize the differences in the sounds. Naturally, the child who has been exposed to word games, books, and magazines in the home would be more advanced than the child who has not had experiences in visual and auditory discrimination.

Girls usually acquire ability in visual and auditory discrimination of words better than boys. Girls are about six months more mature than boys at six to eight years of age; therefore, the girl who has average intelligence is a little more ready to read in the beginning of the first grade than a boy of the same age with the same intelligence quotient. Research has not indicated why boys are slower in developing certain abilities in preschool experiences. It would appear that girls spend more time in quiet play that may involve reading and observing word forms, and in playing word games. Boys are more restless at this age and will not sit still to listen to stories or engage in word games. They do not appear to be as interested in the printed word when they are young as girls are.

INTEREST IN BOOKS

An interest in printed words and books is important to the success of the first-grader in reading. Also important is the ability to maintain attention in a reading situation. These two qualities are often cultivated in the home. The child who has not had the opportunity to cultivate an interest in printed words and has not been helped by his parents to maintain attention in the reading task finds himself in an awkward predicament. The child who is eager to learn to read and write long before the first grade is the one who generally does well.

GRADES

Even when a child is not ready to learn to read in the first grade and does not learn to read well, he should never be given an F in reading by his first-grade teacher. This is one of the most devastating and traumatic things that can happen to a young child. An F in a subject in most cases does no good whatsoever. The best grading system for the first grade allows the teacher to indicate where the child is reading. For example, if he is in reading readiness, then RR is marked on the report card. If he is in primer 1, then P^1 is marked on the report card. If he is in the first half of the first grade, then 1^1 is marked on the report card, and so forth.

There are many tests that determine whether a child is ready to begin reading. Naturally these tests are called *reading readiness tests*. Most of them are of a general nature; they measure background skills and usually predict success for children who come from middle- and upper-class homes. Reading readiness tests are seldom predictive for children from culturally deprived homes. Very often the children who come from the lower classes and who are culturally deprived will have a negative score on reading readiness tests and will show no signs of being ready to read in the first three or four months of the first grade. In many cases they suddenly blossom out and become good readers, eventually catching up with the rest of the class.

INFORMAL TEST FOR READINESS

It is true that words and letters look very much alike to a young child; therefore, exercises for the youngster can point out whether he is ready to read. Parents can play a role in determining the child's reading readiness. One good exercise is to type the alphabet in capital letters on one side of a page and in lower-case letters on the other side. Determine if your child can tell the diffrence between the Capital R, for instance, and its counterpart in lower-case letters, which of course would be the small r. A five-year-old who can reproduce the letters or find any capital letter and then point out its counterpart in lower-case letters is showing good signs of readiness. Another good method of identifying whether the child is ready for reading is for the parent to print the child's name on a sheet of paper and have the child copy his name beneath it. If the child can print the name in a readable way, he is well on his way to being ready to read.

Parents can also utilize a little exercise in auditory perception to determine if their child is ready to begin reading. For example, the parents may list a group of words beginning with the same letters, include one word among the group that does not begin with the same letter, and ask the child to tell them which word is different from the others.

The parents can pronounce five words with letters beginning and sounding alike and have the child pronounce them also. They can then ask the child if there is a word among the group that begins with a different sound. The parents again pronounce the same five words and again ask the child if there is a word that is different. Of course, the correct answer would be "no." Parents can also list a group of words beginning with a letter such as *c* and ask their child if he can hear the *c* at the beginning of the word. Later they can use a list of words ending in *s* and ask the child if he hears the *s* at the end of the word. Examples could be *cookies, carrots,* and *apples.*

Parents can also cut out animals and paste them on paper, pasting the words identifying the animals beneath them with the first letters missing. The parents then ask the child to tell them what the first letter is that identifies the animal. For example, beneath a picture of a cow the parents print *ow* and ask the child which sound and letter the word begins with. Hopefully, the child will say *cow,* and the parents will then ask the child for the letter. Whether or not the child knows the letter, the parents write the letter beneath the picure.

If the child does well on these exercises by the age of six, his parents can assume that he is ready to read. If he cannot do well on the exercises listed above, then his parents should practice more with him. However, they must remember to place very little pressure on him and to make the situation a pleasant one and not one that will be traumatic or destroy his love for learning.

The exercises mentioned above are to let parents know if their children are ready to learn to read. They are not the reading readiness exercises for which the teacher is responsible in the first grade; they only exist to help the children of parents who are interested in teaching them to read. This readiness test should be considered supplementary to the first-grade program.

If by the time a child enters first grade he cannot carry out the exercises mentioned above, his parents should alert the teacher and tell her that they will work with her in any way that they can to help their child learn to read. The parents should not suggest to the teacher that she is supplementary to them but should make it plain that they are willing to help her in any way they can.

LANGUAGE GROWTH

There is a very close relationship between reading ability and language growth. The child's language training begins the moment he hears a spoken word. Through the process of constant repetition, he begins to associate certain words and sounds with things that happen to him. Later he attempts to reproduce sounds he has heard and gradually develops an understanding of language.

Few parents realize that language, oral or written, forms the cornerstone of their child's education and that from this cornerstone of language skills rises a structure that will consitute his education. This language is the beginning of reading, and reading is the basic tool for all learning.

The preschooler is primarily a self-centered person. Language provides a means by which he gets what he wants. While he is getting what he wants, though, he is learning to associate symbols with objects. This association of language is the essence of reading.

A very important factor that affects the language development of children is the socioeconomic status of the family. It appears that our society presently supports the language development of children who have a high socioeconomic status. This is also true of learning to read. It appears that children from the higher socioeconomic levels learn to read much faster and much better than those from lower levels. This is all associated with language development: children from the lower socioeconomic levels do not hear the same language as children from the middle and upper classes and are not allowed to see the same things. Children from the lower socioeconomic levels use fewer words, use less mature sentences, have greater difficulty in interpreting the language of others, and generally have poorer articulation. The greatest degree of language sophistication is found among the children of professional people.

As can be seen from the above statements, a readiness program is imperative for the child from the lower socioeconomic level if he is to achieve proficiency in reading. This is generally not done in the home because parents are not interested; teachers should be cognizant of this fact and give more attention to the children from lower socioeconomic levels in order to enrich their experiences.

Learning to communicate is an accomplishment that is markedly affected by the child's environment, and the environment in which he is reared before coming to school is dependent to a large degree on the social and economic status of his parents.

READINESS—A PERSONAL MATTER

Readiness, like ability, is a highly personal matter. The child should be his own motivator. Usually, he will be if he is not hampered by a great number of restrictions placed on him by well-meaning parents and other adults who think that by structuring his play they will lead him in the direction in which they want him to go. It seems not to matter to the adults that it may not necessarily be his way of developing. Children will develop at their own speed and in their own way with much greater efficiency; the sooner adults realize this, the better it will be for the child. Some parents rush and push their children too much. They do not let them enjoy being children.

Individual differences that are inherent in the child should be considered first. A child's personal growth curve gives a very good indication of his readiness for school subjects. The child who grows slowly may not be ready at the same time as another child the same age, but that does not mean that he will not attain the same level of achievement at a later date.

We all agree that all children do not learn in the same way. A child may not be ready to function in an accepted way, but he may achieve as much in an unorthodox way. If he is continually thwarted and made to do everything in a conventional manner that is foreign to his nature, he may give up the struggle and regress to a state of permanent unreadiness. He may also lose whatever creative ability he possesses.

Chapter 4

READING AND CHILD DEVELOPMENT

JUST as individuals learning to drive a car are at first concerned and preoccupied with the mechanics of shifting the gears and turning the wheel just enough to go around a corner, a child at first is concerned with the mechanics of reading. Starting at the left and going across the line, starting at the top and going down, differentiating *cat* from *dog*, and remembering the sounds of letters are some of the mechanics of reading.

Later, just as individuals learn to drive without a conscious effort, a child will develop reading skills that become seemingly automatic, until he reaches a point where he can read almost any word he sees without having seen or heard it before.

Reading is more than just making sounds that match symbols. Symbols are nothing until they mean something to somebody. So the words a child reads must have meaning for him. Written words come alive when a child sees them under a colorful picture of a familiar object or when he sees his name over the locker where his coat hangs or on his possessions. He lives his words as he counts out paper for each child or distributes the drinking straws at milk time.

He was reading when at the age of four or five he selected his favorite record from a stack of eight that all had the same red labels. He was reading because he was discriminating similarities and differences; he was using certain clues to recognize the object for which he searched. When a child reads from the printed page he is using similar clues, except that they are more abstract and subtle.

Reading, then, is the process of securing meaning from printed words. It is a key that unlocks doors. Doors of self-esteem, peer-acceptance, new information, recreation, future happiness, and success are opened in proportion to the reading skills the child possesses.

Being ready to read does not happen as soon as the child enters school. He has been working toward this goal in language development since his birth.

Reading is a developmental process. Growth enlarges without a noticeable change in complexity. When something grows, it stays the same except for getting larger. Development, on the other hand, indicates a sequential unfolding and gradual change in complexity. If they are begun at the right time and with the necessary essentials, reading and child development will occur simultaneously and painlessly. As the child develops physically, mentally, socially, and emotionally, reading takes its place at the proper time.

Studies in child psychology suggest that there is a time in a child's life when he is best able to acquire a certain skill with ease and assurance. The best time for learning to read appears to be at about the mental age of six and one-half. Some call this the "teachable" time. Before that time the child's efforts to learn reading skills will often end in defeat or frustration. Parents should know that mental age and chronological age are two different things. Mental age is determined by the intelligence quotient, or IQ. For example, a child whose actual age is six and who has an IQ of 120 has a mental age of seven.

Newborn babies are totally dependent on human care, but they have natural ways of responding to experiences and to the care they receive. They cry and make random movements in an effort to get relief from hunger, cold, or pain. As these instinctive acts are reacted to by the mother, the infant gradually learns to modify his ways and conform to a model. So the child is experimenting, and he is also learning from these experiments. As learning continues, the child develops language. New concepts are based on older ones. Random movements gradually become deliberate motions. Instinctive sounds give way to consciously controlled sound productions. The child, then, begins to imitate the sounds he hears. At about a year and a half he can use tonal inflections effectively even though his speech sounds are not clear yet. Gradually, by listening and differentiating he learns phrases and sentences. Slowly he develops a vocabulary. These skills carry over to more complex language learning and to reading readiness. Language and the motor involvements that go along with it are the foundations of reading readiness. *Inner language,* the child's association of objects with their uses, develops first. *Listening language,* the child's understanding of the words said to him, then begins to evolve. Inner and listening language develop simultaneously until *spoken language* appears. Inner, listening, and spoken language continue to develop as the child matures. Oral language development must precede reading readiness. Most children develop language in relation to their social, emotional, physical, and intellectual development.

The child's first year is one of rapid physical growth. His weight doubles in five months. His brain increases 130 per cent in size. During this first year muscular movements develop from automatic reflexes to grasping movements, crawling, and perhaps walking. Emotionally, the child reacts to the feelings of his mother. He smiles at two months and cries almost from birth in an effort to have his needs attended to. He becomes a social creature at about the age of six months and begins reacting to other children. His intellectual development is measured by his language development. At two months his breathing rhythm may cause random sounds. The vowel sounds are first to come forth; this is called *cooing.* Shortly after this stage, all the sounds in the language may be observed. The child does not yet know which language he will speak, but later he will imitate his parents. By six to eight months he can control the sounds he makes and entertain himself by repeating or babbling them. His mother steps in at this time and repeats the sounds to him; he responds with more of the same, and imitative speech begins.

From one to three years of age the child grows fast physically, but at a slower rate than during the previous year. His brain increases about 25 per cent in size. By thirteen months the child is usually walking. Emotionally, he emerges from an egotistic state to a friendlier attitude by the age of three. He moves from jargon to speech and uses his new-found skill for social control. He enlarges his vocabulary, and his sentences become more complex.

From three and one-half to six years the physical growth pace slows. By the age of five most of the gross motor skills such as running and jumping have been mastered, and handedness is fairly well established. Socially, a child in this age bracket begins to develop group identity, because now he is having more association with children his own age. The average child improves his speech sounds, knows about 2500 words by sound, uses longer sentences, and likes to dwell in great detail on events he has experienced.

This natural developing unfolds smoothly if the child has adequate brain, nervous system, and muscle control. In addition, he must have an accepting and stimulating environment where he has a chance to have new experiences, someone with whom to identify, and someone to love him. A vital part of the unfolding process is the element of time. The child needs to be given time to mature and to learn, because rates of development vary in different children.

Language is made up of gesturing, listening, thinking, reading, and writing; each of these develops according to the individual.

All knowledge comes to a person through his senses. They are his contact with the world around him. Hearing and vision are the most important of the senses, especially for learning to read. Sensory growth is related to general physical growth. Some children's eyes may not be ready to do close work that requires both eyes to work together until about the age of eight. The child needs not only the ability to see at a distance, but depth perception and near vision as well. Some research suggests that the immature eye can be damaged when it is taxed to make the sweep from left to right in reading a line of print. There is also some research indicating that this is not true. There are more cases of nearsightedness in the upper grades than in earlier grades, but this does not indicate that those children affected may have started reading too early.

The child must be able to distinguish one sound from another and to follow verbal instructions in order to develop skills in reading. He has to be able to combine a sound he hears with a symbol he sees and then combine that with other symbols to form a word. This is quite a complex problem for any child.

Some studies suggest that visual and auditory discrimination, seeing and hearing similarities and differences, may have more bearing on reading ability than mental age. Most authorities agree, though, that mental age is the most important thing in being ready to read. The majority of first-graders know the meanings of the words they are taught to read, so beginning reading instruction stresses discrimination of auditory and visual likenesses and differences.

Auditory discrimination is more important for words that are spelled the way they sound. Visual discrimination is relied upon heavily for reading words that are not spelled according to the way they sound. Auditory and visual discrimination play a tremendous role in reading ability but do not alone guarantee success in reading.

Mental maturity is another vital factor for reading success. As stated previously, the consensus is that a mental age of six and one-half is recommended for beginning reading. With most children, mental development is related to their age in years. For some it is ahead of their age in years and for others it is behind their chronological age.

Good body concept is a must for reading. A child needs to know how his body looks in order to read. He must know that he has two hands, two eyes, two legs, etc. He should know his left from his right, since he has to learn to move his eyes from left to right.

The child's self-image (his feeling about himself) is another important factor. This is closely related to his emotional development. He must feel worthwhile, capable, acceptable, and loved in order to be successful in reading. If he has a secure, accepting home and school atmosphere, his emotional development should be no problem.

There are several factors, then, that are important for developing reading readiness: emotional security, a mental age of six to six and one-half years, fluency in speech, skill in listening and following directions, social adjustments, an interest in pictures and books, physical skills in eye movement, visual discrimination, auditory discrimination, and a desire to learn to read. Readiness, however, does not end when the child reads his first word. Readiness for learning at each new level of development must continue throughout the school years. As the child develops and as reading tasks develop, all the areas of readiness play their part.

From the ages of six to eight, children begin to use finer muscles than they did before. Holding a pencil, using scissors, and looking at small print are some of the finer muscle activities the child develops. At this age girls are about one year ahead of boys in physical maturity. Parents should also be aware that girls are generally ready to read about six months before boys. Mentally, these children are ready to begin the developmental task of reading. It is a task that will require years of practice and guidance in order to reach their maximum potential. Socially, these children are becoming less self-centered and more group-centered, and they interact better with adults.

The reading program may be a phonic approach where the sounds of letters are learned before words are presented; a look-say approach where a basal reader is used to introduce familiar words, gradually adding more words and longer sentences; a linguistic approach where the use of the word and others like it are introduced and increased in number; or a special alphabet approach where each sound has only one symbol to represent it and transition is made later to the regular alphabet. There is no one best way to teach reading. The important thing is that the child beginning the task of reading should be mentally, physically, emotionally, and socially ready with the added ingredient of motivation prompting him.

At about nine to eleven years girls are still ahead in physical development. During these years children's interests begin to widen. They like to read for information. It is said that people read more between the ages of eleven and twelve than at any other time period in their lives. It is about the age of ten or eleven, at the end of the fourth grade, that the reading programs shift from reading instruction to using reading as a tool for getting information. Children who have not developed in reading as rapidly as they should often find that they begin to have trouble in school for the first time. Some children will need instruction in how to read for information at this time.

From the ages of twelve to fourteen children move into puberty. They undergo physical changes at different rates. They are growing fast and may be clumsy because they do not have full control of fast-growing muscles. Mentally, they move on to the tasks of organizing facts and using reading as a tool. They are very self-aware and are conscious of what others their age are doing. The social events that become important at this age crowd out much of their pleasure-reading time; however, children this age are emotionally sensitive and are influenced by what they read.

The development of a child's reading ability is gradual and continuous. Most children go through the same patterns of development, with their reading ability emerging in an orderly sequence. Although this development is orderly, it varies in rate within a child and from child to child. There are differences in the ages at which children are ready to begin developmental tasks such as walking, talking, and reading. The pattern of a child's physical, mental, social, and emotional development is related to his success in reading.

Reading is a developmental task; this means that it is a task a child must perform in order to satisfy his needs and the demands of society, and that his accomplishment of the task enhances his total development. There is a time when reading should begin. If it is not begun at that "teachable moment," it becomes harder to master. The farther the learner gets from the teachable moment, the harder it is to learn the task.

Maturation is a ripening process, and parents should know that pushing the child and trying to "hurry up" readiness will not help him. When he is ready to learn to read he can be taught. There are many readiness materials available for working with children, and they should be utilized. But the child should not be pushed too hard, because he may not be ready.

Once he is ready, his parents still should not push him too hard, but should be patient. In addition, they must know their child's emotional makeup and the basic foundations of the reading process.

Chapter 5

CAUSES OF READING PROBLEMS

Y OUR son may come home someday with a poor grade in reading. Of course, it may be your daughter, although research has shown that boys have more reading difficulties than girls. This is due to several factors. Boys are usually slower to mature than girls; they have greater motor drives, and they are usually more aggressive. Also, our society puts more emphasis on boys "being boys" and on girls making good grades.

Naturally, you are worried by this reading failure and find it hard to understand. The purpose of this chapter is to help parents and teachers gain a greater insight into why a child may have a low achievement in reading.

It has been reported that the incidence of serious reading difficulties is as high as 30 per cent of the school-age population. That would mean that almost four million children have serious reading problems.

Sixty per cent of a given elementary-grade class will fall below grade placement on a standardized reading test.

For many years it was believed that seriously retarded readers had some sort of brain lesion. It was not until the early part of the nineteenth century that this theory was exploded. Authorities protested vehemently and research indicated that many, many causes of reading retardation existed. Since the early 1900s, research has found even more causes of reading difficulties.

Research studies have revealed that a great many factors can contribute to failure in reading achievement: poor vision, poor hearing, poor speech, poor teaching, inadequate schools, or an inferior environment. Other suggested causes are aphasia (word blindness), minimal brain damage, gross brain damage, emotional maladjustment, and low intelligence.

When a child displays a reading difficulty, his parents usually think first of a vision problem. If a survey were to be conducted of children with reading problems, it would reveal many visual defects. Reading places a great deal of strain on the eyes; therefore, the child with poor eyesight certainly could have difficulty in reading. Even a slight defect will cause fatigue if reading is done for long periods of time. Many parents cannot understand their child's disinterest and low achievement in reading and protest that he has had an eye examination at school. This may be true, but the eye examination was probably a test like the popular vision chart test, which only reveals symptoms of myopia (nearsightedness); other visual difficulties are often overlooked. These visual defects are too numerous to list. If your child has a reading problem, it would be advisable to take him to a reputable eye specialist. The child who continually blinks, frowns, holds his book close to his face, loses his place, rubs his eyes, or is tense during visual activities should have an adequate eye examination.

To learn to read well, it is essential that your child have the ability to hear sounds accurately. A great many school children—perhaps 5 per cent of the population—have a serious hearing loss. It is also apparent that a great many others have a slight or moderate loss. It is evident that since a great deal of basic reading instruction is oral, a child who has a hearing loss has a good chance of becoming a reading disability case. It is likely that your child will be given a hearing test when he enters school, but his defect may still be overlooked and remain undiscovered. Symptoms of hearing impairment should be recognized early. If a child often appears inattentive and disinterested, it may be because he does not hear what is said to him. If he constantly asks to have things repeated and does not seem to understand simple directions and instructions, he should be given a hearing test.

Closely associated with hearing impairment is the problem of poor speech. To learn to read effectively a child must have an adequate command of his language. Poor speech habits and poor pronunciation habits should be discouraged. Parents should not allow their children to indulge in baby talk. Many parents allow their child to speak in this manner because they think that it is "cute." The child will probably have trouble when he enters school and attempts are made to alter his speech patterns. Indistinct speech can prove to be a hindrance to reading because the child cannot make the correct sound when he views a letter. It is often difficult to determine whether the difficulty lies in loss of hearing or in poor speech habits. Usually the latter is the case, and these poor habits should be corrected. The child who has a speech defect will almost certainly have many emotional maladjustments relating to the problem if it persists. The child may be afraid that the teacher or the children will laugh at his mistakes when he reads aloud. Too often this is not his imagination. This makes him very self-conscious, and he may refuse to read aloud or even to talk in class. Since this embarrassment occurs most often during reading activities, his resentment toward reading may be great. These resentments usually spread to silent reading. Therefore, the emotional disturbance caused by defective speech can be a very large factor in reading problems.

Health problems are often contributing factors in reading disabilities. As stated previously, learning to read is not a simple task. To learn to read well a child must be alert and attentive. Chronic health problems that reduce strength, vitality, and the ability to concentrate are often the cause of retarded reading. When a child is not feeling well, he does not learn as quickly as he should. He misses a great deal of what is being taught, and this, of course, hinders his progress in future years. A child who has poor health is likely to miss a great deal of the instruction in basic reading skills. He is at a loss when he returns to school and often becomes discouraged. Unless some remedial instruction is given either at home or at school, he will be well on his way to becoming a disabled reader.

Minimal brain damage is sometimes thought to be a cause of reading difficulty. This type of brain damage may occur at birth or at any time afterwards. Evidence taken from a great many studies seems to indicate that too much emphasis is being placed on minimal brain damage as a cause of reading problems. *Dyslexia* is a term often associated with poor reading and minimal brain damage. This term can be defined as the inability to read when the child has normal intelligence, proper instruction, and a good home environment. This child is usually able to perform well in tasks that do not involve reading. *Dyslexia* is a vague term, and it is not always possible to diagnose a child with this anomaly accurately. However, we do find children with average or above-average intelligence who have attended good schools and still do not read well.

Another condition that is sometimes recognized as a cause of reading difficulty is congenital word blindness. This type of word blindness is present at birth. The child cannot recognize word forms; he can see black marks on the printed page, but does not recognize that they stand for words. When he tries to read it is almost as if an American child were trying to read Chinese. A child may have symptoms similar to those caused by word blindness when it is really a case of immaturity. It is very difficult to distinguish between word blindness and immaturity.

Intelligence is often considered a factor in reading problems. However, every child can be taught to read. Children with low intelligence will learn to read at a slower rate, but they can and should be taught to read. Naturally, the degree and level of comprehension vary with intellectual capacity. Even an educable mentally retarded child (IQ 50 to 75) can learn to read at a fourth- or fifth-grade level.

Mixed lateral dominance is sometimes offered as a possible cause of reading difficulties. In this condition a child does not favor his right or left side consistently. The role that lateral dominance plays in learning to read is a very controversial one. A child who has mixed lateral dominance may write with his left hand, look into a microscope with his right eye, and kick a ball with his right foot. Many studies have been done to discover the role that this condition plays in reading disabilities. Some authorities argue that reading difficulties are more likely to occur in children who have mixed lateral or crossed dominance, while others say that there is no relation between lateral dominance and reading disabilities. If one considers all the research conducted in the past seventy years on mixed dominance, the conclusion must be drawn that it has little to do with reading difficulties.

A child is said to be ready to read when he has matured at all levels. He is said to be intellectually mature enough to read when he has achieved a mental age of six and a half years as indicated by an intelligence test. He should be able to communicate effectively, have an adequate command of oral language, and display an interest in reading. However, intellectual maturity is not the only factor to be considered in reading readiness. The child must also be socially and emotionally mature. If a child is exposed to a learning experience before he is ready for it, he will be unable to handle the situation.

There are a great many things that parents can do to help their children become ready to read. When your child comes running into the house to tell you about something exciting that he has seen, don't ignore him. Listen carefully, and encourage him to use complete sentences. Utilize every opportunity you have to increase your child's vocabulary. Give your child pictures and books to look at, and read aloud to him as often as you can. Also, teach him to identify sounds. This can be done by encouraging him to listen to all kinds of music. In addition, it is also important for him to know how to follow directions.

Reading difficulties may be produced by a number of different factors. Sometimes they result from overprotective parents. The child who has had everything made easy for him may become discouraged if he finds that it is not easy to learn to read. Reading can be an arduous process, and many children do not know how to exert the effort it takes to learn. A child may expect the story to come from the printed page as quickly and easily as it does from the television set. When it does not, he may become discouraged and refuse to try to learn, or he may become extremely nervous when he is called upon to read aloud. If the retarded reader's parents are too severe in their discipline, he may be unable to learn because he is afraid of being a failure. A child's ability also may be stifled by parents who are never satisfied with his work. No matter how well he does they say that he could have done better. Other parents are indifferent to their child's progress, and, of course, no one likes to be ignored. If no incentive is given, it is easy for the child to give up and not care about learning to read. Many parents put too much pressure on their children. They become extremely anxious, and this anxiety is conveyed to the child. He feels that he cannot meet his parents' expectation; therefore, reading difficulties occur.

Observation of the behavior of disabled readers in comparison with the behavior of children who are progressing well reveals that they differ in how well they are adjusted socially and personally. Retarded readers are characterized to varying degrees by tenseness, withdrawal, anxiety, aggressiveness, and resistance. There also appears to be a circular effect in which the reading disability causes an emotional problem and the emotional problem in turn brings about increased anxiety about reading. Therefore, the personal and social adjustment of a child is linked closely to his emotional adjustment. Many children with symptoms of emotional disturbance learn to read well and do not become reading disability cases at all. Therefore, neither parents nor teachers should consider that the emotionally disturbed child will necessarily be a reading disability case. But it can be pointed out that most children having reading problems are also nervous and anxious.

An inability to learn to read well generally causes severe frustration for the child. His unsuccessful attempts to read make him conspicuous, and he feels ashamed. He has a continued lack of success and constant frustration; therefore, he has severe feelings of insecurity. Many such children become easily convinced that they are dumb. Unfortunately, this feeling is often enhanced by the attitudes of their parents and even the teacher. Therefore, for the child, reading becomes even more disliked, and he seeks opportunities to avoid it. Everything that this type of child does leads him to believe that reading is something to be disliked; this becomes a vicious cycle. These children often resort to excessive daydreaming or nailbiting, and are often sick in the morning in order not to go to school.

Research has shown that family conflicts are greater in the

homes of poor readers than in the homes of children having no reading problems. It has also been found that parents of poor readers tend to use derogatory terms concerning their children and also tend to devaluate their abilities more than the parents of good readers do.

The child who is happy and well adjusted, and who feels loved by his parents, is more likely to make adequate progress in reading than the child who feels insecure and feels that his parents are not giving him a fair chance.

It is often disastrous to a child when his reading achievement compares unfavorably with that of a sister or brother. The inability to compete successfully with a brother or sister is likely to develop a feeling of extreme inferiority. In an attempt to cope with this feeling, the child often refuses to compete or try to keep up with the other child.

It is extremely important for the child to develop favorable attitudes toward reading. Favorable attitudes foster progress in learning to read, while unfavorable attitudes result in reading disability. The home is the first place where favorable or unfavorable attitudes are nurtured. In most cases, though, unfavorable attitudes toward reading develop after the child begins school rather than before.

THE RESPONSIBILITY OF THE SCHOOL

To a very large degree, proficient instruction in reading depends upon the ability of the teacher. It is true that it is the responsibility of the school to develop a happy, well-balanced child. But it is also true that the teacher has the responsibility to teach the child the most important tool in his life—reading.

Too often the child is started in the reading program before he is ready to read. The next year he is promoted to another reading level when actually he was not ready to leave the first level at the end of the school year. Thus, the child drops farther and farther behind in the reading process, and no one in the school situation seems to care or know how to remedy the problem. There is no doubt that the school can be a vital factor in promoting good reading; it is also a chief factor in causing reading disability.

Chapter 6

WORD RECOGNITION AND COMPREHENSION

READING is one of the major concerns of the schools and the parents of today. By the time a child enters the fourth grade, he has to contend with reading not only a basal reader, but also health books, science books, and music books, to name but a few. The farther along the child progresses in school, the more reading he will encounter. If he gets a slow start in reading or if he lacks in one or more of the important reading skills such as word recognition or comprehension, he might easily become overwhelmed by the increasing amount of reading required of him.

As parents, you naturally feel that the school would be responsible for preventing reading difficulties in your children. When reading difficulties do occur, you expect the school to overcome them. However, when you know that each teacher usually has from twenty-five to thirty-five or more students, you realize that part of the burden of helping your child to read must fall to you as parents.

The task is twofold. First, you must provide the child with the necessary experiences that will enable him to successfully accomplish a task as complex as reading. Second, you must be willing to help the child who already has encountered a problem in reading. However, it does not matter whether you are trying to prevent the problem or solve it; the reading skills with which you need to become familiar are the same. These skills will fall into the broad categories of *word recognition* and *comprehension*. They are the ones that your child must master in order to become a good reader.

Under the major headings that follow, both readiness and remedial activities will be discussed in relation to the various techniques that can be used to develop recognition and comprehension.

WORD RECOGNITION

The most basic of all the reading skills is word recognition. This may be defined as the ability to recognize or identify the sound (pronunciation) and meaning of a word when it is seen. The child must not only recognize the word the first time he sees it, but he also must be able to identify the word each time thereafter. If a child lacks competency in word recognition, he cannot read.

Word recognition is not taught through any one means of attack. There are several methods, and the child should be sufficiently exposed to each so that he can choose the technique that will help him identify words rapidly. Care should be taken not to place too much emphasis on any one technique, such as phonics, since this leaves the child without any means of identifying words that cannot be broken down phonetically.

Let us examine the different techniques used in word recognition.

Basic Sight Vocabulary

Generally, upon entering school a child develops what is called a *basic sight vocabulary*. This is a group of words the child can recognize immediately without the use of other identification tactics such as context (using the sense of the sentence to find word meanings) or phonics clues. A child who does not have a large enough sight vocabulary will spend so much time trying to recognize new words that he will not be able to understand what he is reading.

Preschool Activities

One means of developing a basic sight vocabulary for your child is to take blank cards approximately 3 x 8 inches and print, in small letters, the names of common objects that can be found around the house (see Fig. 2). It is important that your printing

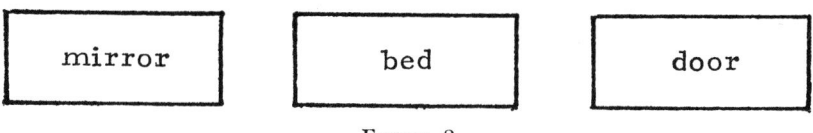

| mirror | bed | door |

FIGURE 2

be similar to the print your child meets in his reading book. If you are not sure how to correctly print certain letters, check a handwriting manual that has the alphabet in it. When the cards have been printed, tape them to the appropriate objects and call your child's attention to the fact that the letters on the card mean the same thing as the object to which the card is taped. Begin with two or three cards and increase the number gradually as the child progresses. After the cards have been up for about a week, take them down and tell your child that the two of you are going to play a game. Mix the cards and ask the child if he can look at a word and match it correctly with the object it represents. If he succeeds, praise him and add another card for the next week. If he fails, you can help him to rematch the cards correctly. Do not make any remarks concerning his failure. Instead, say something like, "That was a little too hard for the first time, wasn't it? Let's put the cards up again, and this time we'll look at them real hard so we can match them the next time we play the game."

Another project you and your child could work on together is making a picture book. Purchase a scrapbook and urge your child to cut pictures from old magazines to paste in the book. Print, in small letters, the name of each object beneath its picture. This is an excellent time to introduce verbs into his sight vocabulary, instead of using only nouns. A picture of an animal running can be used to identify the verb *run*. Pictures can be found to illustrate other actions, such as *sit, jump, walk,* and *climb.* The backgrounds of action pictures should be uncluttered to avoid confusion as to what the word represents. Your child will be proud to have a book that he can read "all by himself." When he has become thoroughly familiar with the book, spend some time with him, covering the pictures, to see if he can recognize the word when it has no connection to the picture. Also, encourage your child to make up sentences using the words in his picture book, since isolated words will have little value to him. You may want to use a published list of basic words as a guideline to the types of words your child will be expected to learn once he enters school. The child's teacher can tell you about several of the popular word lists. You may find them at local bookstores, too.

Sight vocabulary words can also be taught incidentally. For example, while traveling, call your child's attention to words on signs along the side of the road. He may pick up words such as *stop, eat, danger,* and *yield* that are basic to everyday travel. Do not underestimate the power of television commercials and ads on cereal boxes—they often succeed when other methods fail.

Remedial Activities

If the informal inventory reveals that your child has too small a sight vocabulary, then exercises that require rapid reading should be used to overcome this problem. Be sure to use a basal reader at a level that is easy for your child to read. If you have a workbook available, you can use all the exercises in it that require new vocabulary words to be read as whole words and can avoid those exercises that require difficult word analysis. When a workbook cannot be obtained, you can prepare homemade games that use the vocabulary from your child's basal reader level.

A game like Words will be enjoyed by most children. The whole family can play this game together with a maximum of enjoyment and a minimum of trouble. Cut several pieces of cardboard five inches wide and six inches long. Randomly place the desired words on the boards as shown in Figure 3, allowing a free space in the middle of each board. On small pieces of paper make a copy of each word you use along with one of the five letters shown. Buttons or pennies may be used as playing pieces. Play the game as you would a game of Bingo. (You

Word Recognition and Comprehension

W	O	R	D	S
this	down	many	that	where
see	who	all	come	saw
when	two	FREE	went	most
what	why	upon	some	those
less	got	came	to	them

Game board

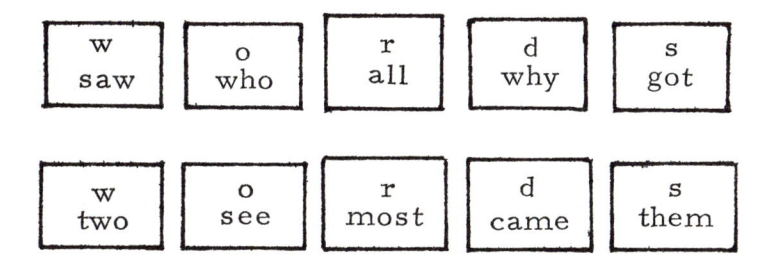

w saw	o who	r all	d why	s got

w two	o see	r most	d came	s them

Pieces of Paper

FIGURE 3

call a letter and word and the child places the button or penny on the word on his game board.)

Younger children (five and six years of age) will enjoy fishing for words. Attach paper clips to the backs of word cards and make a fishing pole with a magnet tied to the end of the string. If your child can read the word he catches as soon as it is fished out of the "lake" (a pan or bucket of water) he may keep the word. If the child has to study the word in order to be able to read it, he must throw it back into the lake to be caught another time.

PHONICS

Phonics is another technique that is used by children trying to recognize unfamiliar words. It is the ability to associate sounds with the letters or elements of the words they represent. As a child advances in school, he is introduced to phonics skills at increasing levels of difficulty. Phonics is usually begun by familiarizing a child with a certain word in his basic sight vocabulary. For example, if he knows the sounds of the word *an,* he can figure out such words as *fan, can, man, ran,* and *pan.* Next the child becomes acquainted with the consonant blends (*br, ch, pl, tr,* etc.) and the long and short vowel sounds. Practice in these skills is continued throughout grade school. Parents can help by making up games that utilize these sounds.

Preschool Activities

Before a child can successfully utilize phonics to unlock words, he must have a background in auditory discrimination, which is the ability to hear likenesses and differences in sounds. Playing rhyming word games with your child will help to increase his facility at hearing likenesses in sounds. Differences can be practiced by having your child repeat patterns which you sing: alternate both fast-slow patterns and loud-soft patterns. Car rides provide an excellent opportunity to play these and many other games with your child which you might not otherwise be able to include in a busy schedule. It is also to the child's advantage since he will not usually have as many things to distract him as he does at home.

Commercially produced listen-hear records are available that enable your child to look at a book while the story is being read on the record. This gives him practice in careful listening as well as in following directions so that he will know when to turn the pages of the book. If you and your child made the picture book described earlier in the chapter when the basic sight vocabulary was discussed, you will find that it can also be used for phonics work. Call your child's attention to the beginning letter of each word and the sound it represents. See if he can name other words that begin with the same letter. If he can, you might want to print some of these words on the back of that sheet to use as new vocabulary words.

Remedial Activities

Although your child may need a great deal of remedial work in phonics, it may be in only one phase of the program. When the difficulty lies in an inability to sound initial consonants, a device such as the one shown in Figure 4 might be used. Several of these devices could be made using different word families, such as *ake (make, bake, lake)*, *ook (look, book, cook)*, or *all (wall, fall, hall, tall)*. The initial letters are placed underneath each other on the sliding strip. As your child correctly identifies a word, have him use it in a sentence to demonstrate that he understands its meaning.

For use in reinforcing blends, the slido-letter can be modified by placing the blend to the left of the sliding strip and the various word endings on the strip itself (see Fig. 4). Other blend combinations that could be used besides the one shown are *bl (blue, black, blank)*, *ch (chair, chin, chop)*, or *tr (tree, trip trot)*. In this case, the final letters are the ones that would appear on the sliding strip.

Many types of exercises can be used for teaching vowel sounds to your child. One exercise is to list words with double vowels in which the first vowel is long and the second is short, such as *beat, meal, boat, people* and *road*. Have your child list the long vowel and then use the word in a sentence. A second exercise is to make up sentences with a word missing and then to provide three answers in parentheses, telling the child to choose the word that has a short vowel sound. An example would be: "The little boy stumbled over the —————— (stone, rock, toy)." Other exercises can be found in the workbook at your child's reading level.

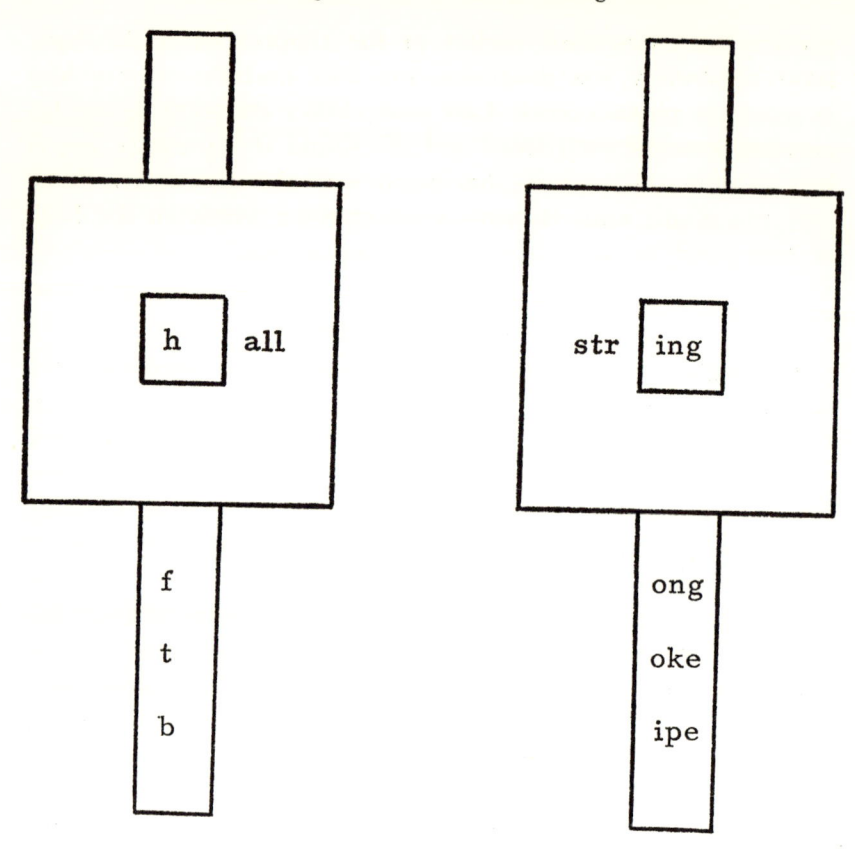

```
         h  | all              str | ing

         f                         ong
         t                         oke
         b                         ipe

      Slido-letter          Modified Slido-letter
```

FIGURE 4

CONTEXT CLUES

Proficiency in the use of context clues is one of the most important word recognition skills a child can develop. It provides for rapid and immediate word recognition through understanding other words in the phrase, sentence, or paragraph. In a sentence such as, "The man put the hat on his ———," the child who is reading for meaning will be able to identify the word as *head* without any difficulty. Besides enabling a reader to recognize words quickly, context clues also serve as a check on other word recognition techniques. Suppose that a child reads a sentence as, "See the horse," instead of "See the house." A glance at a picture above that sentence might show the child that *horse* could not be correct because it has no connection with the picture. The two examples illustrate the two types of context clues: verbal and pictorial. A child beginning school is primarily exposed to pictorial clues in his books, but as he gets older and the pictures in his books become fewer, he must rely on verbal clues.

Preschool Activities

A young child must have an adequate listening and speaking vocabulary before he can successfully handle context clues as an aid in word recognition. Parents should read books to their child in order to supply him with experiences that he might not get otherwise. Many, many types of books are available for less than fifty cents that will enrich your child's listening vocabulary as well as his speaking vocabulary. As you read to your child, point out the action in the pictures and question him about what he thinks is going on or what he thinks might happen to the characters in the story.

Other activities include making up simple riddles that your child can answer, such as "What animal has four legs and purrs?" and playing a sentence completion game in which you make up sentences with a word left off at the end that your child can complete. Examples might be "A cow gives us ------," "We buy milk at the ------," or "The little girl put the shoes on her ------."

Remedial Activities

As stated previously, riddles may be used to help the school-age child develop contextual skills. You might want to write the riddle out with several answers, then have him read it and choose the correct answer. Or, you could take sentences from his reader, leaving out one word that he can identify from the context of the sentence, giving several words to choose from; for example, "Hal went fishing in his ------ (jeep, boat, house," or "Susie blew out the —————— on her birthday cake (icing, diamonds, candles)." If your child is younger and having more problems with picture-context clues than with verbal-context clues, you could make a book with pasted pictures, writing sentences beneath these pictures with a word missing. An example would be: "The dog is —————— (eating, running, sleeping)." To correctly answer this statement, your child must refer to the picture.

STRUCTURAL ANALYSIS

Skill in structural analysis is the ability to recognize root words and to interpret the new words they have formed through the addition of letters before or after the root word. Prefixes are additions to the beginning of a word that alter the word's meaning *(happy, unhappy; head, ahead)*. Suffixes are additions to the end of a word that alter that word's form but not its meaning *(walk walking; laugh, laughing)*. In compound words, the child must identify smaller words within a large word. Compound word exercises also fall under the heading of structural analysis *(someone, everybody, Saturday)*.

Preschool Activities

Activity for the young child in this area will consist mostly of learning to note likenesses and differences in objects. For example, set up a row of three red blocks in front of your child. Behind this row set up three more red blocks but add a white one. Ask your child how the two rows of blocks are alike and then what it is that makes them different. This exercise could be varied by using different objects and by gradually making the differences harder to see.

Remedial Activities

Exercises to improve structural analysis skills could largely consist of lists of words with differing prefixes and suffixes. Have your child draw a circle around the root word in a list of words; for example; *seeing (see), plays (play), helper (help)*. With words that have prefixes such as *mis* or *re,* ask your child to explain how the prefix makes the word different and have him use it in a sentence. Lists can also be utilized for practice in finding the smaller words that make up larger words. Have your child draw a line separating the compound word into its smaller units (*tree/top, dash/board*).

DISCRIMINATION CLUES

A child who uses discrimination clues is trying to unlock a new word or to discriminate between two look-alike words. Similarities and differences are important with this type of recognition technique as is the shape of the word. Words such as *what, when* and *where* may appear very much alike to a child until someone points out to him the differences by drawing lines around the words to indicate their shape (see Fig. 5).

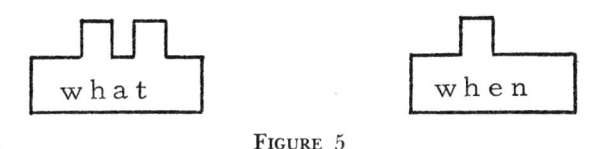

FIGURE 5

Preschool Activities

One thing in which a child is interested at this age is himself and his friends. Let him draw the shapes around his name and the names of his friends, and then compare them with each other. Let the child point out the differences and likenesses.

Remedial Activities

Concentrate on having the child draw shapes around words and identify similar and unsimilar parts of these shapes. Work with words that your child confuses with each other. This will help him to pay more attention to details in look-alike words.

DICTIONARY USE

When a child encounters a strange word that does not reveal its identity by any other word recognition method, he should be able to go to the dictionary to determine its pronunciation or meaning. If possible, every home should have a dictionary. Picture dictionaries are available for preschool and early school-age children and, of course, standard reference works are available for older children.

Preschool Activities

Naturally, for your child to be able to use a dictionary easily, he must be thoroughly familiar with the alphabet and the position of the letters in it. You could make a game of this by printing each letter of the alphabet on a different slip of paper, or on cardboard if you want it to last longer, then having your child arrange the letters in their correct order. Begin with only three letters and work up to larger groupings as the child seems able to handle them. When he becomes fairly proficient in this task, let him cut pictures from magazines to start a picture dictionary. He may want to cut out several pictures for each letter or perhaps only one. A scrapbook may be used with one or two pages allotted for every letter. Print a large capital letter at the top of each page and print the names of the objects in small letters underneath the pictures.

Corrective Activities

The child who needs work in using the dictionary often benefits from playing the alphabet-arrangement game as described under preschool activities. Listing words for him to put in alphabetical order will also help. When he is skilled in alphabetizing words with different first letters, you should present him with lists of words having the same first letter. Next, progress to words with the same first and second letters *(already, although, also).* Let him see how quickly he can find words in the dictionary and time him, making a game of it. Encouragement and practice are perhaps the most important elements in this area.

Although, as a parent, it is natural for you to want to help your child as much as possible, there are certain things you will need to remember. For the parent of the preschool child, it is well to keep in mind that not all children are ready to read at the beginning of the first grade. In fact, some may not be ready for reading until the second or even the third grade. Whatever activity or game, then, that you try with your child, you must watch for signs indicating that the activity is too difficult for him. This does not mean that you should give up trying to prepare your child for school, but rather that you might have to delay some activities for a period of time. During the time that you and your child are working on an activity together, do not be afraid to discontinue it if he expresses reluctance to continue or if he tires. It is best to end an activity while the child is still interested. Don't forget, most often your child will tire of something before you will.

It is especially important for the child already in school not to feel pressured to catch up to his classmates in reading. More than anything else, your child needs encouragement and the feeling that you have confidence in him. Always begin any work that you do with your child on a level that is easy enough for him to experience success. Also, guard against expecting miracles overnight; occasionally this does happen, but more often than not, progress will be slow and, hopefully, steady.

COMPREHENSION

Even though in this chapter comprehension is being treated as a separate topic, it cannot be divorced from the development of word recognition. Every word that a child learns to recognize should have meaning for him; in return, word recognition and identification techniques must be spontaneous in order for the child to comprehend the words adequately. Provided that he has developed adequate word identification skills, the child should be able to comprehend a selection as well in written form as he can in spoken form.

Because your child may be able to read a paragraph beautifully, word for word, do not automatically assume that he understands what he has read. A child may even remember what he has read and be able to answer certain questions without actually getting the true meaning. Suppose that your child has just read a story about raccoons being night animals, and you have questioned him as to what type of animal a raccoon is. He may be able to answer by telling you that a raccoon is nocturnal; to most people this would constitute a correct answer, but we need to dig further to check his understanding. Ask him what *nocturnal* means—then you will know whether he fully comphehends or is merely repeating words.

There are many aspects of comprehension, such as reading to get the main idea, selecting outstanding details, summarizing and organizing, arriving at ideas, following directions, predicting outcomes, and reading graphs and maps. Although your child may be poor in one of these aspects, this does not necessarily mean that he will be poor in all areas of comprehension. The child who cannot follow the train of thought in a paragraph or story may still be able to get meaning from a single sentence.

In addition to the many aspects of comprehension a child must master, he also must contend with certain other factors that can hinder his ability to understand what he has read: whether or not he is interested in the reading material, the difficulty of the material, adverse physical conditions, and personal handicaps. Physical factors may interfere with a child's ability to gain comprehension more than most parents realize. If a child is overly tired or thinking about how hungry he is, he cannot concentrate.

Parents should set a bedtime for their child and stick with it to insure that he gets the proper amount of sleep each night. You know that you cannot do your best work or housework if you do not get adequate sleep the night before, and this goes double for your child. Also of importance is a good breakfast. Other physical factors to consider, especially as your child advances into the upper elementary grades, are such things as adequate surroundings and proper lighting. Even if your house is crowded with other children, space can be found for a small table, chair, and lamp in the corner of some back bedroom.

Children must first learn to comprehend words, then phrases, sentences, paragraphs, and finally longer selections. We will now see what can be done to help improve your child's skills in each of these areas except for individual word comprehension, which was covered in the section on word recognition.

PHRASING

In order for your child to understand more quickly what he is reading he should read in thoughts rather than word by word.

Word Recognition and Comprehension 69

This means that he must pay particular attention to punctuation for proper emphasis and voice intonation. Improvement can be brought about by encouraging your child to read aloud, being careful to watch for each punctuation mark. His phrasing ability might be increased by making up multiple-choice questions with phrases as answers; for example, "The whale swam (a) over the mountain, (b) in the ocean, (c) over the ground." Flash cards can also be used that make a complete sentence but forces the child to read it in thought units; for example, "See Dick—go—to town—on his bike."

SENTENCE COMPREHENSION

You can help your child increase sentence comprehension by underlining part of a sentence and having him tell you whether it tells who, what, where, when, why, or how. An example of each follows:

1. The goat is *in the meadow* (where)
2. *Hal* went to school. (who)
3. Put the *book* on the table. (what)
4. Lana came home *early yesterday morning.* (when)
5. *Because she was hungry,* Wendy ate six biscuits. (why)
6. Susie went *by car* to visit her aunt. (how)

PARAGRAPH COMPREHENSION

Paragraph comprehension is the ability to identify the topic sentence, which is the sentence containing the main idea of a paragraph. You can give your child practice in this by having him choose the best title for a paragraph or by having him devise a title of his own that describes what the paragraph is about. A variation of this is to have him cross out the one sentence in a paragraph that does not belong. Exercises of this sort can be found in workbooks written for your child's reading level.

COMPREHENSION OF LONGER SELECTIONS

The child should first learn that there are three main parts to a story: the *introduction, body,* and *conclusion. His* parents can help him look for these parts and know the purpose of each. You can help your child by asking him definite questions about what he has read or by writing questions that he answers as he reads. Again, exercises can be found in various workbooks that will help a great deal.

Please remember that comprehension should not be considered separately from the other reading skills. It should be developed in conjunction with the other skills as an ongoing process from the first grade into the higher grades.

Be patient and understanding with your child, help him as much as you can without pressuring him, and allow him to progress at his own rate, and you should be able to develop an adequate reader.

Chapter 7

YOUR CHILD'S INTEREST AND TASTE IN READING

MOST parents are concerned with their children's reading ability and the progress they make in reading. All parents want their children to be able to use their education to the best of their ability when they reach adulthood. Parents should realize that their children's ability or inability to read will affect, to a great degree, their present and future achievements in life.

What then can you do in your home to help your child develop his reading interests. Most authorities agree that a parent's greatest contribution to his child's reading program is made by promoting more and better reading in the home. As has already been discussed, your child begins to develop attitudes toward reading very early in life. This means that his reading attitude, interests, and tastes are first learned in the home.

Your child comes to school with his own unique ability to learn to read. All children are different; therefore, no child shares the same ability with another child or develops at the same rate. The school depends on you as a parent to provide your child with a variety of experiences to support the reading programs taught in the school. Even if your child does not have a reading problem, the school still depends on you to furnish supplementary materials that will interest your child and help him to become a better reader. Only a parent can provide an atmosphere of lifelong enjoyment of books. Such experiences as a family reading hour, a story-telling hour, and other similar events will help your child develop a respect and love for books.

There is a difference between interest and taste. In this chapter, when the child's interest is mentioned, we mean that he enjoys a certain subject when he reads. For example, he might like to read adventure stories or animal stories. When the child's taste is mentioned, it refers to a certain quality of reading material in the area of his interest. For example, he might read a comic book or he might read a higher-quality book about adventure, animals, or science fiction. In other words, he can be reading low-quality, middle-quality, or high quality material concerning the same interests.

Parents must be careful not to think of the child's interest only in the area of fiction. The child should also become interested in other reading, such as historical and biographical material, scientific material, and material from many other fields. Not only should you try to develop the child's interest in many subjects but at the same time you should improve the quality of the material he reads. There are many factors that play a part in the development of your child's interest and taste in reading. These include your attitude as a parent toward reading, the attitude of the general public toward reading, the child's leisure-time activities, the availability of good material, the age and sex of your child, and his intelligence.

Perhaps one of the most important factors in the growth of your child's interest and taste in reading is your attitude toward books. When you first began reading to your child, his reading interest and taste started to develop. There are some children who come to school having seen only the Sunday comic page and a few low-grade story books. On the other hand, there are children who have been read to many times from high-quality children's literature. These children have the advantage of being familiar with good reading materials.

You child's habits, attitudes, interest, and taste in reading are further developed during the elementary school years. Whether good or bad, these qualities stay with him throughout his life.

Very often without realizing it, a parent will indicate to his child that he has a poor attitude toward reading. When a parent has not found reading to be of any great personal value, he may feel that his child is wasting his time or being "lazy" when he reads. Often, the parent will ask the child if he has nothing better to do than read. Or he may order the child to get up and do some chore so that he will not be wasting his time reading books. Situations such as these only let the child know that the practice of reading is not very acceptable at his house. He may soon become unwilling to be caught reading at any time. Needless to say, this is very bad.

It is not only your attitude as a parent that is important to your child's interest and taste in reading, the attitude of the general public toward worthwhile literature also influences your child and helps determine the quality of his interest and taste.

Current happenings also help to shape your child's interest in reading. What happens today helps to form the reading interest of your child's tomorrow. For example, space flight and the landing of men on the moon have generated a great deal of interest in science and aviation material. The amount and kinds of recreational and learning activities that are available outside of school help to determine your child's reading interests and tastes. For example, leisure time, play, television, movies, sports, music and art lessons, and Boy Scouts and Girl Scouts take up a great deal of your child's time. However, these activities, as a whole, are worthwhile and profitable for the child. While it is true that your child has many demands made on his time, it is very likely that he can find time to read if it is made attractive to him. Your task is to guide your child toward a balanced program of activities.

Still another important factor in the development of your child's interest and taste in reading is the amount and quality of the reading material available to him. Your child may not be reading material that is particularly interesting to him. He may be reading the material he finds at home even though it is not his favorite type. You as a parent can provide interesting, high-quality material for your child to read at home.

The age and sex of your child are of great importance in determining his interest and taste in reading. The young child (three to six years old) likes stories about animals, stories concerned with fantasy, and fairy tales. By the age of eight the child has begun to develop an interest in realistic or real-life stories. Boys begin to read stories about dramatic action and adventure. Girls begin to read stories about home life and school. Around the age of ten, boys and girls develop different interests in reading. About this time, other activities begin to take up much of a child's reading time. Even though the amount of reading done by the child of this age tends to decrease, he still should have a certain interest and taste that continues to develop.

In the junior high school years, the sex differences in reading continue to be evident. A boy usually prefers to read stories about space and aviation, science, and adventure, and, to a much smaller degree, stories about animals.

On the other hand, girls are most likely to want to read romance stories, poetry, stories of home and family life, and an increasing amount of adult literature. Most boys and girls dislike subtle humor or descriptive stories. However, simple mystery stories that involve young people and patriotic stories are very interesting to boys and girls of this age.

Biographical and historical materials appeal to junior high school boys and girls who have average or superior reading ability. They will often prefer to read a story of this kind that deals with a character of their own sex. Although a girl may read a story that would be of interest to a boy, it is rare that a boy will be found reading a book that is considered to be of interest only to girls. Generally, during the freshman year in high school, the amount of reading done by your child will decrease considerably as social interests and sports participation take the place of the youngster's former reading activities. This trend may continue into the early college years.

Your child begins to mature in his reading taste when he becomes a senior high school student. Both boys and girls become interested in reflective, artistic, and religious literature. Interest in the areas of science fiction and the supernatural decreases at this time. When boys and girls become adults, the differences in their reading interests lessen, and it eventually becomes a matter of their individual personality and taste instead of their sex.

A child of less than average intelligence tends to like fewer subjects and may read inferior-quality books. For instance, he may prefer a comic book or a picture book about the classics. At the same time, a child of average or above-average intelligence might prefer to read a higher-quality library book.

Perhaps the least important factor in shaping the interest and taste of your child is the "look" of the book itself. The color, binding, pictures, and size of a book are more important to a younger child than to an older one. An older child is more concerned with whether he enjoys a book than with the way it looks. However, poor readers dislike big, thick books without attractive pictures. Even though the looks of a book aren't as important to the child as the type of story contained in it, this factor cannot be overlooked. It is especially important to present an attractive book to a poor reader.

Now that we have considered the factors that determine your child's interest and taste in reading, you will want to know how you can use this knowledge to help your child become a good reader. There are several ways parents can do this.

First of all, you will need to check with your child's teacher. She can help you guide him toward a balanced, interesting reading program. The teacher may prefer that you don't try to teach your child to read. She may even say that this hinders the reading program at school. However, you will be helping your child to develop his reading skills if you encourage him to enjoy reading more.

Both you and your child's teacher can benefit from parent conferences, home visits, and parent-teacher meetings. The teacher can inform you of your child's reading progress in school and can suggest good-quality materials on many subjects that he may read at home. On the other hand, you can supply the teacher with your child's present interest and taste and with his reading progress at home.

It is not enough for parents to know their child's present interest and taste in reading; they must also know and understand the level of his reading ability. The fastest way to kill your child's interest in reading is to give him material that is too difficult for him to read.

The higher-quality books on any subject usually require a greater degree of reading ability than those of lower quality. If your child does not have the necessary reading skills for a certain book, you must not expect him to be as interested in it as he is in material that he can read easily, even though the latter may be of poorer quality.

There may be times when it is hard for you and your child's teacher to find books of high quality that your child can read easily. This is the time to look to the school librarian for guidance. The teacher and the school librarian should have expert knowledge of children's books and their level of readability and can often help you to locate these materials. However, this does not mean that your child has to read only those books that are easy for him. It does mean that he should not be given reading material that he cannot read with a reasonable amount of effort.

It is very important for you to realize that your child's reading level does not stay the same. As he reads about more subjects and uses higher-quality material, his reading level is raised. You can keep informed on your child's reading progress by talking often with his teachers concerning his current reading level and by observing him at home.

As stated previously, a good way to help your child progress in his ability to read is to take him to the public library. Let him have his own library card. He will soon realize that the library has many interesting books for him to read.

It cannot be stressed too strongly that you should share books and experiences with your child. Encourage him when he shows an interest in books and reading. Often a smile or a word to the child will help him, especially when he first begins to read independently. To develop the practice of reading, work with him often and answer his questions.

Once you have considered the factors that influence your child's interest and taste in reading and his reading level, you are ready to begin helping him. With this knowledge you can make the best use of your time and abilities to help your child develop the habit of reading and enjoying good books.

Chapter 8

STUDY SKILLS

IT is quite normal for a parent to have high expectations for his child in school and then to receive a report card and find that all his aspirations have been in vain. Although parents are often quite biased, in many cases they can predict if their child is bright enough to be an average student. Many times when these predictions are totally wrong the difficulty lies not in the child's inability to learn but in his inability to read.

Today many parents are confused and angered by their children's failure to read. As stated previously, problems in reading come from many sources including poor teaching by the classroom teacher, very little help or encouragement from the home, and poor study skills on the part of the student. A parent can do very little to remedy the first factor, but he can easily correct the second one if he puts his mind to it. However, the third factor depends upon the cooperation of all three: teacher, pupil, and parent. You, the parent, might ask, "What do I know about study skills?" or "How can I help Johnny or Susie become a more skillful reader?" Although it may sound confusing at first, once you know what study skills are and how they help in the overall picture of reading, you will be able to help your child develop better habits in reading.

Study skills are often defined as habits, attitudes, and states of mind that improve the ability to study. For example, working in a quiet place, budgeting time, doing an assignment correctly, and concentrating during study are cited as skills that help the pupil make the most of his reading time.

Study skills in reading are the skills used by a pupil when he must do something with what he is reading. Common reading skills include selection and evaluation, organization, recall, location of information, and following directions. In using the skills of selection and evaluation the child must pick out the most important parts of the assignment. That is, he must judge each item and decide whether it is related to whatever he has been asked to do. He has much more to do than simply recognize words. Finding the main idea in a paragraph is a selection and evaluation study skill. The child must consider all the ideas in the paragraph and then decide which is the most important. Organization of the information he has gained through reading requires the pupil to put together related items that belong in the same category. A successful student must recall what he has read—that is, he must fix the information in his mind in order to remember it when it is needed. To do this, he must locate the needed facts while he is reading instead of memorizing many items. The basic point is that the pupil must understand the material he reads before he can recall it. You, the parent, might help at first by telling him which sentences are important and why.

Locating information is very important to becoming a skillful reader. Children must be able to find page numbers quickly, locate certain sentences to check answers, use a table of contents and index correctly, and be able to use encyclopedias and almanacs To be good at these skills the pupil must use the library; therefore, he should have good library manners and know how to care for books.

Following directions is a very important skill that is needed in studying all subjects. Most assignments are given in the form of oral or written directions Students who have difficulty in understanding the directions for their reading should have these directions repeated several times, written down if possible, and practiced often. Parents can help by giving several types of directions at home that require their child's undivided attention to follow them.

All of the common reading skills point to the fact that getting the meaning is basically what counts in reading. To be successful, children must read with full understanding.

In addition to the large common reading skills, other small

study skills can be considered in clusters or small groups. For example, an outlining cluster might include reading for details, finding the main ideas, changing the main ideas to phrases that contain the most important information, and using an outline form acceptable to the teacher. To use these smaller skills to the greatest advantage, the child should follow the steps to determine the main idea of what is being read.

The first step would be to find the key words in each sentence. The child must decide what the main ideas are and must remember the details. The second step is to find the key sentence in each paragraph. This is done by adding up all the main ideas to see if they are contained in one sentence. The third step is to determine the main thought of the paragraph. If there is no key sentence, the student must look at all the important ideas.

There are three main types of reading ability that underlie the basic reading study skills. To guard against weaknesses in study abilities, the school program should provide for all three of these types. They are *thorough reading, skimming for review purposes,* and *reading for details.*

Careful, thorough reading is necessary for success in most school subjects. This type of reading is used to acquire basic information and an understanding of the facts that form the background and enhance the plot of a story. In order to do this type of thorough reading, the student should master the study skills of paying attention to what is read, organizing ideas, and understanding what he reads silently. The goal of this type of reading is to remember the most important ideas in an organized and accurate way. If a pupil can become a thorough reader, he should have no difficulty with such reading skills as selecting the main ideas, organizing ideas, and following directions. Parents can help their child strengthen this skill by having him read one paragraph at a time from a story and then tell them the main idea contained in that paragraph. The child can also be given several short sentences, some of which contain major ideas and others minor ideas, after which the child must determine the differences between the two.

Parents should help their child read the headlines of a newspaper and then compose his own to cover a story or happening. It is most important for parents to encourage their child and help him to develop thorough reading. Almost everyone comes in contact with situations where he must follow directions exactly, select the main ideas from a story, or get very detailed facts concerning a situation.

In many school situations partial reading, or skimming, is necessary. Skimming is used to locate an exact piece of information in a paragraph and to refresh one's memory about certain events. It is used for two purposes: to locate specific information easily and to classify information.

Skimming to locate material does not call for speed when the student is first learning. Afterward, though, with practice he can develop speed.

Another use for skimming is classifying materials. Reading and deciding quickly what things go together often increases the child's speed of reading.

Reading for detail is learned last because it involves skills at a higher level than the ones used for thorough reading and skimming. In this type of reading the child pays a great deal of attention to his own thinking and to the specifics of what he reads. Also, in this type of reading the child must associate meanings. The next few paragraphs are concerned with reading for detail.

THE INDEX

Skills in using the index of a book are needed to help your child find information on a certain topic. He must be familiar with these skills in order to locate certain pages. If he is, he will be able to save time and eliminate the problem of thumbing through the book and possibly never finding the information for which he is looking.

In order to use the index skillfully, the child must know what it is and where it is located. Naturally, this will vary with the type of book. To look up a subject in the index the child should know its "key word." Also, when using the index of a book the child must be able to find a word quickly in a list arranged in alphabetical order. This skill can be mastered with practice and patience.

READER'S GUIDE

The child needs to learn to use the card catalog and the children's card catalog in the library. The *Reader's Guide* is very useful in helping children locate magazine articles and appriate material.

Reader's Guide—A reference souce to periodical literature indexed by subject headings

Card catalog—A listing by title, subject, and author of all the books found in the library

Children's card catalog—The same as the card catalog except that it pertains only to children's books

OUTLINE

It has already been stated that it is very important for your child to see the relationships which the author intended his ideas to have. A good outline of the reading material is an excellent representation of the essence of the material. When this outline is studied, the ideas stand out and are quickly recalled, and their relationships with each other are readily observed. This is a very effective way of reviewing certain materials.

An outline is a simplified version of the author's work. Words or groups of words are used that mean the same thing as the author's ideas, rather than using the total number of words and sentences found in the story.

In making an outline, the child must (a) choose the main topics, (b) choose the subtopics, and (c) write in correct form the words or groups of words that represent particular ideas. Below you will find an illustration of an outline in its correct form.

SUBJECT OF THE SELECTION

I. Statement of the main topic
   A. Statement of the first subtopic

      1. First detail
      2. Second detail
  B. Statement of the second subtopic
      1. First detail
      2. Second detail
      3. Third detail

This illustration indicates the use of only one main topic. The same form should be used with each remaining main idea. The next statement of the main topic would be listed under Roman numeral II. Its subtopics would be written as illustrated above.

ATMOSPHERE FOR STUDYING

It is the duty of the teacher to see that the classroom atmosphere is one that lends itself to a good studying environment, and it is your responsibility as a parent to see that the same type of atmosphere is available in the home. A child cannot be expected to apply study skills effectively if he is constantly so distracted that he is unable to concentrate.

The child should have a particular place set aside that he knows is his "studying place." Naturally, it should have proper lighting and a comfortable chair where he can sit. Notice that the word *sit* was used and not *recline*. The study area should be away from all distracting sounds, such as television or other family activities.

Study skills, which have been discussed in this chapter, can be applied to reading in or out of the classroom. The teacher is in control of the reading situation while your child is at school with the exception of the time he spends in the school library. The child who has little or no desire to read anything in addition to the material he must read in the classroom has not developed the broad interests in reading that he needs to be a whole person. Therefore, your role at home in teaching your child to read broadly is a very important one.

HOMEWORK

Except for developing study skills, homework is seldom effective. An elementary school teacher has approximately thirty students in her class. In order for homework to take care of individual differences, the teacher would have to assign thirty different homework lessons. This is not feasible from the viewpoint of designing the homework lessons or of grading them. It would be effective if the teacher could divide the class into four homogeneous groups and give four different homework assignments. This would be a tremendous job, however, from the viewpoint of developing and grading the assignments.

If the homework takes care of the gifted child, it will miss all the rest of the children in the classroom. If the homework assignment challenges the slow learner, it will miss 80 per cent of the children. If it challenges the normal or average group, it will miss 50 per cent of the children. When the assignment challenges the bright child, then of course it will miss the gifted, average, and slow learners. From this discussion it can be seen that homework is not effective in developing concepts or in supplying new knowledge to the child.

In the third grade the teacher should give some homework that will develop study habits for the child. The parents are instrumental in developing these study habits and should see that their child does this homework adequately and that it is handed in on time. Again it must be pointed out that this homework is building study habits, not doing a great deal to add to the child's knowledge.

The elementary school child has so many things to do that homework encumbers his activities to the point where it does more harm than good. In many cases the child wants to come home in the afternoon and play and should be allowed to play, but instead he is given homework to do and then perhaps dancing lessons, music lessons, or other lessons until it is time to eat. Most children would like to watch television after the evening meal and should be allowed to, but if they are encumbered with homework and piles of assignments from the elementary school, all they can do is work, work, work—usually at what is just busy work.

Parents expect their children to have homework because they

remember their own education, and they had homework. It should be pointed out, though, that education today is different from the education of thirty years ago and that it is much better now. The child who does not have homework in the first and second grades is lucky, and the child who has a little homework in the third and fourth grades to develop study habits is also lucky. He is even more fortunate if his parents help him to build study skills.

Chapter 9

CHILDREN WITH LEARNING DISABILITIES

W HO is the child with learning disabilities? He belongs to a category of exceptional children that is easier to describe than to define. This child's problems are called by many names, but the two most prominent are *special learning disabilities* and *communication disorders*. His learning difficulties are often described in terms of characteristics that may not apply to him: mental retardation, blindness, cerebral palsy, deafness, or faulty instruction. Children with learning disabilities have been described as educationally retarded, dyslexic, autistic, emotionally disturbed, neurologically disorganized, and aphasic.

In this chapter the terms *dyslexia, learning disabilities,* and *communication* disorders are used synonymously.

Regardless of the lack of agreement about definition, the child with learning disabilities is probably best described as one who manifests an educational discrepancy between his mental capacity for learning and his actual level of functioning.

The difficulties of the child with learning disabilities are usually attributed to damage to the parts of the brain that regulate the way an individual "sees" things after his senses have presented the facts to him, and to damage to the parts that control his movements and his impulses. This child is usually retarded in one or more of the processes of speech, language, reading, writing, arithmetic, or spelling.

The child with learning disabilities who has above-average intelligence has baffled parents and educators for years. This child is often referred to by teachers as immature, a slow learner, undisciplined, or emotionally maladjusted. Parents have considered him lazy, hard to control, scatterbrained, or just highstrung. These disturbances prevent or impede a normal learning process.

These perceptually handicapped children have been pressured by their parents and teachers, and failure has been more the rule than the exception. They are often on the defensive and many feel quite hostile toward their parents and teachers. The behavior of these children makes many of them as unacceptable to their peers as to adults. The behavioral patterns most frequently seen are a short attention span, distractibility, hyperactivity, and impulsiveness.

One of the most obvious of the difficulties that are characteristic of the child with learning disabilities is his distractibility, or oversensitivity to stimuli. The normal child usually inhibits his response to stimulating situations and his overt behavior is not intense. The opposite is true of the child with learning disabilities. His activities are very intense, he responds to many stimuli, and he expends a great amount of energy. He seldom stays still.

When this child changes from one activity to another, he shows a tendency to be preoccupied with repetition of the former activity. This perservation is another of the obvious characteristics of the child with learning disabilities, whether they are minimal or major, and even if no brain damage is involved.

This child's bizarre behavior and inability to learn in the traditional classroom are usually the forces that instigate parents to take the first steps toward seeking help.

The financial status of the parents is a governing factor in determining the procedure. Probably the best and least expensive diagnostic facility available is a publicly supported child guidance clinic. Here a team approach is provided. Psychiatrists, psychologists, neurologists, educational consultants, speech therapists, and pediatricians correlate their findings for a diagnosis and treatment.

Referral to the clinic is usually made by the teacher. Before the child is seen, a school report is obtained from the teacher, a social worker, and the guidance counselor. A developmental history must be obtained from the parents, and later the child and the parents are called in for interviews.

At the clinic various psychological and educational tests are administered to the child. The complete Wechsler Intelligence Scale for Children (the most popular individual intelligence test used in America), the Bender Visual-Motor Gestalt Test, and a reading evaluation are necessary for the preliminary evaluation.

Our concern in this chapter is with reading disorders that result from a dysfunction in the brain. For the purpose of this chapter we will call this condition *dyslexia*. The child suffering from dyslexia scores average or above average on intelligence tests, but cannot read at the proper level.

Generally speaking, dyslexia is considered more than just a reading disorder. It is a part of a language and learning disability that rarely occurs in isolation. For example, the child who has a reading disability very often will also have a communication disability and learning disabilities in other school subjects.

A child normally learns an adequate listening language by the age of six; when he enters school, he learns to read by utilizing his hearing and seeing language to interpret symbols. Reading, therefore, is another step in the total language process. After the child acquires a certain proficiency in recognizing symbols he is ready for instruction in writing. Later he will learn arithmetic, and most dyslexic children generally also have some trouble with arithmetic. However, these children do better in arithmetic than in reading, writing, or spelling. There is an old saying that if a child has a reading deficiency, it will be exaggerated in the fourth and fifth grades. This is very true, because at about this time in the child's life, he begins subjects such as history, geography, and literature that require a great deal of reading. If he cannot read adequately, then he cannot gather the facts, and he will become a failure in school.

Children with learning disabilities very often have trouble learning to distinguish right from left. This problem then complicates the reading process, because in learning to read the child must learn to go from his left to his right and from the top of a page to the bottom.

· Since spelling involves many skills, including auditory and visual discrimination and memory, the child who has a learning disability very often is also a poor speller. As can be seen, the child who is dyslexic will probably have trouble not only in reading, but also in arithmetic, writing, spelling, and, later, the content subjects.

It should be pointed out, though, that if the child is given immediate attention in the first grade, he will have a much better chance of being an average student than if this condition is determined later in his life.

REMEDIAL EDUCATION

Remedial procedures for dyslexic children should be based on the findings for each child. It is fairly difficult for parents to try to help a child having learning disabilities, by studying remedial procedures of a general nature because the diagnosis is complicated and each child will require a different technique. The teaching for this type of child should be an individual thing—one teacher for one child. It is a long drawn-out process and parents should not expect overnight results. Generally speaking, the dyslexic child is discovered in the fourth or fifth grade. It has taken approximately ten or eleven years for the child to get in this predicament. Therefore, it is illogical to assume that he will overcome his deficits in a month or even in six months. With good corrective teaching, though, the parent should see considerable improvement in six months to a year.

HOW, WHEN, AND WHERE IT HAPPENED

Parents are often stunned when they are told that their child has learning disabilities or communication problems. This initial shock is quite understandable, for their problem is a real one. Most parents begin to wonder how it could have happened. They mull the situation over and over in their minds but generally come up with no solution.

There are few data on the causes of learning difficulties in children to give direction to parents and professional people concerning these children. While scientists understand a great deal of what may happen to the fetus as it develops in the mother, they do not know yet how to prevent damage to the unborn child. There is a possibility that learning disabilities are caused by something that attacks the brain during pregnancy. There are many viruses the mother can contract while pregnant and transmit to the fetus that could cause learning disabilities. We could explore at least three hundred causes of these problems, but that is not the purpose of this chapter. Let us say then that learning disabilities can be caused by many factors.

This condition is discussed in this chapter because invariably children with learning disabilities have reading problems. If these children are average or above average in intelligence, the problem is compounded; they know that they are different, and their parents know that they should be learning. The children are faced with failure every day of their lives, and they know that they are failing. This is a heavy burden for any child to carry. Parents should not put the blame on their children but should seek help from the best professional people available in order to help them overcome the deficiency.

The child with learning disabilities is almost always a discipline problem. This is particularly true if he is a boy. Because he is a discipline problem and is often being punished, he usually does not get the attention he needs in the regular classroom. The child who is kept out of the classroom as a punishment is missing excellent instruction which he should be getting. Too often this child is placed in a special class for the mentally retarded because he is a discipline problem and not because he has low intelligence. This, of course, should never be done. Parents should examine the credentials of the professionals who test their children and should not accept an IQ score from just any source.

The child with learning disabilities looks and acts just like other children. This child may be a very good-looking boy or a beautiful little girl; the problem is not externally visible. It is merely a disorder that does not allow the child to recognize printed symbols. The child may be normal in all other respects but this one.

CORRECTIVE EDUCATION

The teachers of the dyslexic child should become child-oriented and not method-oriented. No one method can deal with all the children suffering from learning disabilities. Each child has a unique problem, which should be treated according to the symptoms he displays. Therefore, no cookbook recipe will handle all the children who suffer from learning disabilities, and no surefire approach will help them all to learn to read. The teacher must know not only the areas in a child that are deficient but also those that are intact and that can be used effectively for learning. The teacher must begin by being diagnostic and must remain diagnostic. If the parent is to help the teacher with this stubborn problem, he too must be diagnostic. The parent needs help in helping the dyslexic child, and therefore he should take the child to a reading clinic. Working with professionals, he can do much to relieve this problem, but he cannot overcome it alone. Parents need a great deal of help from other people, and the child needs a great deal of understanding from the parent.

To indicate how the approach must vary from child to child, let us point out a few examples.

Child A is a young dyslexic with a severe auditory involvement. Corrective instruction begins by giving this child a sight vocabulary and a language approach to learning. Because he is deficient in auditory processes, the teacher will play up his visual processes. For such a child there would be no attempt, or at least only a token attempt, to work with phonics in the initial stage of correction. Gradually, though, from the whole words he learns, he can be introduced to the parts of the words.

Child B is a dyslexic child who has a severe visual involvement and is unable to learn a sight vocabulary that would be classified as adequate. For this child the teacher would begin with an auditory approach. The child could be taught phonic elements including isolated sounds, vowels, and blends, and ways to find small words in large ones. As he progresses, the teacher will experiment in instruction for a sight vocabulary to see how well he can handle it. When he reaches the point where he can handle the sight vocabulary, it can be integrated into the total instruction.

Parents should know that recent research indicates that 95 per cent of dyslexics can learn to read if they are given proper treatment. The outlook is definitely better if the child is identified early in his school career.

MOTIVATION

Most dyslexic children know that they have a reading problem and would give anything to learn to read. Therefore, it is rarely necessary to work on motivation with these children, because they are very highly motivated to read.

COLLEGE

The majority of dyslexics will probably terminate their education at the end of high school because they have not acquired the reading and writing facility necessary to handle the academic work at the college level. This does not have to be. The majority of dyslexics, if they are discovered early enough, could be corrected to the point where they could compete academically with other college students. Many dyslexics do go to college and graduate. Parents of dyslexic children should help their child seek a college that has a good reading clinic.

The author worked with a male student in a college reading clinic who had an IQ of 130. This boy had been in reading clinics since the tenth grade. With much work on the part of the reading teacher, the personnel of the reading clinic, and the student, he managed to graduate from college.

For the dyslexic, speed in reading seems to be a problem. Many of those who bring their comprehension level up to adequacy still find that their reading is extremely slow. This does not necessarily hinder a student when he is reading for such college subjects as biology, history, or psychology. It should be pointed out, though, that most dyslexics are unable to handle a foreign language and are advised not to take these courses in college.

REPEATING GRADES

It is not unusual for dyslexics to have to repeat one and perhaps two grades during their school career. It should be pointed out, however, that repetition of grades is not a good answer to the problem and seldom helps the child. The problem can only be solved through procedures to correct the individual's disabilities.

EMPLOYMENT

Most dyslexics recognize that they are limited in the kinds of employment they can seek and are realistic in their aspirations. Again it should be made clear that if corrective procedures are started early enough, dyslexics should not be limited in the jobs they can seek. On the whole, dyslexics can be self-supporting and economically independent citizens. With the help of their parents and through early diagnosis and corrective techniques, they can become contributing members of our society.

Chapter 10

PARENTS HELP THE GIFTED

GIFTEDNESS has been defined in many ways. Some people put emphasis on measurable intelligence; others on exceptional performance. Some see it expressed in a variety of ways.

Certain characteristics are common to the majority of gifted children. Among these are the following:

1. An early interest in calendars and clocks.
2. High academic achievement.
3. Curiosity, the desire to know "how" and "why."
4. An advanced vocabulary and reading level.
5. A good memory.
6. Superior intellectual ability.
7. Broad interests.
8. An early ability to reproduce a story or event.
9. Good emotional health.
10. A longer concentration span.

Giftedness is usually apparent early in life. There are numerous means available for helping to identify the gifted:

1. Scholastic achievement.
2. Group and individual intelligence tests.
3. Talent hunts in science, art, music, writing, and oral expression.
4. A checklist based on common characteristics.
5. Peer evaluation (from other children).
6. The judgment of teachers.

In the past it was assumed that gifted children would develop their capacities in spite of a poor environment and lack of opportunity, but this is untrue. We now recognize the importance of developing intellectual resources. If these children are to find satisfaction, they need understanding and sound guidance from parents and teachers.

Parents often ask, How shall I help teach reading to my gifted child? One very important requirement is for the parent to know the child's capabilities so that he can honestly make reasonable demands of him. The child fares best who is allowed to be himself; he can then enter more fully into normal contact with other children.

The home has a direct influence on the formation of study habits. Several outstanding boys and girls who were asked whether their parents helped them with schoolwork said that they did, then went on to say that their parents gave help but did not do their schoolwork for them.

The aim of this chapter is to make home training more fruitful in developing your child's interest and talents in reading. Most curriculum differentiation, which the gifted need so badly, must be supplied through their home reading. This is where teachers and parents come onto the scene. Only if children are prepared so that they have the skills necessary to do the most effective job possible can they truly enjoy both the process and the results of reading.

Now that the role of reading guidance in educating the gifted child has been briefly explored, let us examine the various activities and programs that have proved successful in accomplishing this task.

The most difficult problem is to provide enough good reading to satisfy the eager minds of the bright and gifted. An abundant supply of children's literature should be found in every good school library, in the children's reading room in the public library, and in bookstores. Parents should urge their child to join a book club, because this is an excellent source of very good juvenile literature. Books should be given to the child as gifts, selected with the advice of a librarian or of a teacher who knows the child's interests. This is the way to start a home library that will be very useful in the child's reading program.

The child should be encouraged to read many types of books. His parents should hold sessions with him in which he reads aloud to them. His reading skills will improve with daily reading that is tied in with his school studies and outside interests. Like other children, the gifted child needs to practice oral reading in order to have self-assurance when he is called upon to read orally. Reading aloud and holding interesting discussions are ways of teaching a child about life around him. They are also ways of teaching him proper speech. Parents should take the time to listen to their child read orally. For many parents this will present a few problems, but the child's progress in reading should outweight the trouble.

Learning to use the dictionary for word meanings will help a gifted child to read more difficult books. The teacher should demonstrate the use of the dictionary and other reference resources, but parents also need to provide reference resources in the home and to encourage their use.

The reading of biographies is usually a source of enrichment for the gifted child. It has been proved that biographies are a favorite form of reading for the child who has access to the best books of this type. The reading of biographies encourages discussions on the people being studied. Another reason why parents should urge their child to read biographies is because of the insight it gives him into the lives of people with whom he may identify.

The gifted child should be invited by his parents to express his opinion about any of the books he reads. He might also be interested in dramatizations or tape recordings of books to give to friends.

Parents can help teach reading to their gifted child through enrichment activities. Encourage the child to participate in such activities in the following ways:

1. Discuss at home interesting materials that his class is studying.
2. Keep a list of words that are used repeatedly by members of the class. Try to find synonyms and antonyms for the most common ones.

3. Have the child choose a word that may have many different meanings and make up sentences using as many of these meanings as he can.
4. Help select books for the child on major topics his class is studying in social studies, science, etc.
5. Have the child write endings for some of the fictional stories or books that he reads.
6. Assist the child in finding additional works by the authors whose stories or books he reads.
7. Find interesting books that give word derivations and share them with the child.
8. Have the child select reports from a newspaper or news magazine and discuss them orally with you.
9. Ask the librarian to assist the child in learning the most efficient way to use the library.
10. See that the child studies book reviews in newspapers and magazines.
11. Let the child select a recently published book, read it, and write his personal review.
12. Make use of the child's imagination by letting him write his own captions for pictures or conversations for cartoon characters.
13. Have the child make up riddles about characters in stories he has read.
14. Have the child write a story of his own.
15. Let the child try writing poetry for you or for his own enjoyment.
16. Supply the child with crossword puzzles. They are helpful in building vocabulary and spelling power.
17. Have the child write brief biographies about the people in his life.
18. Encourage the child to make up his own tall tales.
19. Have the child write a character study of himself.

In guiding the gifted child in his reading, it is important to encourage him to read mature books and to develop an understanding of good writing and an appreciation for it. Parents should know the various educational levels of books and endeavor to insure that their child chooses a book commensurate with his mental ability.

As parents, encourage your child at a very early age to use the public library facilities, because they can offer adequate, comprehensive, and up-to-date sources.

When possible, purchase a good set of encyclopedias for the home. Many television programs bring up questions which your child can answer from the encyclopedia.

Also, if it is financially possible, the home should have an unabridged dictionary. Many new words that inquisitive youngsters discover cannot be found in standard distionaries. The child should own a good abridged dictionary, too.

There are many reasons why parents should read aloud to their child. It strengthens the bond of family affection, educates the child in many ways, and helps him to develop an interest in many subjects. Have an older child read to a younger child to develop interest for the younger child.

Parents can help their gifted child to become a good reader and a creative reader. They can do this by encouraging the child to do something with what he reads, either at the time it is being read or afterward. Some ways to develop creative readers follow:

1. Reproducing what is read with imagination (have the child rewrite certain pages from a book).
2. Elaborating what is read (have the child give an oral book report to the family).
3. Writing a book report in verse.
4. Writing a movie script for a best-selling book. The child probably will enjoy writing a television play from a favorite short story.

Since your gifted child may already be a good reader, you as a parent should give him encouragement to improve his skills as a creative reader. Try to invent ways of getting the child to do something with what has been read. Five practical suggestions that will help you as parents to set the stage for creative reading and learning are as follows:

1. Encourage the child to be self-reliant. Give him responsibility.
2. Teach him to listen attentively and follow simple instructions and directions. Include him in your conversations.
3. Provide a reading environment and a quiet reading room.
4. Answer his questions or help him to answer his own by relating a new situation to a familiar one.
5. Help him express his ideas orally. Encourage him to use new terms.

To sum up what has been said, it should be stated that reading is one of the best means of broadening your child's background. His special interests will lead him to read books on the topics he most enjoys. Your child should have the opportunity to read newspapers, magazines, and biographies. He should be allowed to share what he has learned from books and what he has enjoyed reading. This can be done in a number of ways, preferably in original ways your child will think of himself.

The key, then, to helping your gifted child in his reading activities is to encourage him to use the books and other materials that are made available to him. Challenge your child even if this means extra work for you. Reading is the tool subject for most of the learning of a gifted child. As parents and teachers, we must make sure that the gifted are being provided with the best possible reading skills. They must also be encouraged to love reading, which will hopefully guarantee that their education will continue as long as there are good books to be read.

It is true that one learns to read by reading. Part of the parent's responsibility is to plant the desire to read, to make reading rewarding, and to insure that the pleasures of reading have at least a fifty-fifty chance in competition with the lures of television and the movies. Thus far in this chapter, we have been discussing what the parents can do; now, briefly, the teacher's role will be explored.

The teacher can assign outside reading in class. The children do the reading outside the class, but it is discussed in the classroom. Doing a book report for extra credit, though, is generally very boring, and students don't seem to get a great deal from it. Instead, the teacher could let the children act out brief dramatizations when three or four of them have read a book or story. The brighter children can also be arranged in small groups for talk sessions concerning shared stories and books they have recently read. The teacher should also encourage art and construction activities that are related to books as well as short stories and other themes. Naturally, children should be encouraged to do creative writing on a suggested topic or on a book they have read. Another very rewarding activity is for the teacher to have the children compile a list of the books they want for Christmas or as a birthday gift. This list can then be sent to parents, aunts, uncles, etc.

The superior child should not just be left alone. All too often this is the pholosophy of parents and teachers concerning the gifted child, and this is a grievous error. It must also be pointed out that we do not want the gifted child to be stereotyped as a bookworm. In all probability this would not happen, but a balance should be encouraged between reading and the other activities in the life of the child. If teachers and parents know that the greatest competition from other areas is at the ages of twelve and thirteen, reading activities at this age can be accelerated.

Although children need the activities mentioned in this chapter it is specifically concerned with the gifted child or the child with an IQ of 130 or above. In most cases these children do well academically and will read everything that the classroom teacher requires; however, for most of these children this is not enough, and other readings should be encouraged.

Chapter 11

ORAL AND SILENT READING

ORAL READING

IN the primary grades oral reading is of major significance, and it is important at all levels when children have reading difficulties. Faulty habits and poor reading become immediately apparent when a child reads orally.

Oral reading also motivates the child to read more. This is seen in the elementary school every day as evidenced by the fact that primary-grade children love to read aloud to a group. The children like to exchange ideas when reading aloud, and it also promotes a feeling of group unity. The full enjoyment of poetry and various types of prose is impossible without oral reading. Oral reading also has many uses in family life, and parents should be encouraged to utilize it more often.

The child who is a poor reader is at a disadvantage in the oral reading group. He should not be asked to read aloud when it might be embarrassing, his oral reading should come at a time when he is alone with the teacher or with two or three of his classmates. At home, though, the parent can tell a great deal about the child's reading ability by having him read aloud passages from a book at his reading level and from one just above his reading level. Oral reading also becomes important as a listening exercise. Children love to listen to stories read aloud to them and enjoy discussing the plot and characters in the story after the reading session. Another important aspect of reading aloud to children is that they can look at their books while they are listening. By listening to the teacher and other good readers in the classroom or at home, the child can learn the inflections used in the voice as they pertain to the printed word. This factor, though, should not be used above the second-grade level because beginning in the third grade most children read faster silently than they do orally. Therefore, requiring them to keep the place in the book teaches then that slow reading is desirable. Looking at the book and keeping the place is only useful to help children learn the inflections that people use for various words. However, children can learn a great deal from listening to the teacher and other children read aloud without following the place in the book.

The teacher or parent should never discuss the plot or the outcome of the book when reading aloud. Interest cannot be expected from the children in an oral reading session when they already know the outcome of the story. A teacher or parent might have the children discuss what they think the outcome of the story will be, then let them find out if they were right at the last reading session.

Carefully planned lessons are important for oral reading sessions because the lessons help determine specific needs. The parent or teacher must give specific attention to the skills basic to oral reading. For example, the volume of the voice is important, as is its flexibility. Enunciation and breath control are important, and naturally the teacher or parent will be able to detect word recognition errors. If this instruction is done at home, the parent and the child should discuss the flexibility of the voice, enunciation and pronunciation, speech control, breath control, and word recognition. If it is done at school, then these topics can be discussed in the group with several children taking part.

The Nature of the Exercises

The exercises for oral reading will depend upon the purpose of the assignment and the needs of the child. The parent should take these steps before having the child read the passage: (a) scan the story and pick out difficult words that may give the child trouble; (b) write down the difficult words and after the child has read the story go over these words with him; (c) ask several questions about the story in order to motivate the child, giving him some of the information he should remember after the story is read to him; and (d) after he has read the exercise, ask him comprehension questions on what he has read.

Reading Drama

In oral reading of drama, each pupil reads the lines of one character. The child will read the entire play while studying his part. In this way he not only reads orally but also learns the content of the entire play. This type of reading can be done at home with the entire family participating or it can be done in class with various children reading the different parts.

Problems of Expression

There are times in oral reading when the parent or teacher should devote his attention to the problem of expression rather than to the facts and meaning of the story. In such an exercise as this, the child will read the passage all the way through; the parent will then read the passage through with the right inflections in his voice, and will ask the child to note his inflections. The child is then asked to read the passage again, after which the child and parent discuss how each of them read the story, passage, or poem.

Phrase Reading

In order for the child to improve in the area of mechanics, which includes interpretation, expression, and voice quality, he should not be timed. Generally, if the child knows that he is being timed, he will become tense and begin to make errors. Phrase-reading exercises consist of listing several phrases on a sheet of paper and sliding a slip of paper with a hole cut in the center over the phrases, allowing the child to see one phrase at a time. The child, of course, is to read each phrase as fast he can.

Occasionally a child reads slowly orally because he is using his finger as a pointer. The phrase drill will overcome this bad habit. Phrase reading is important because word-by-word reading is a slow process, and children should learn to read in phrases rather than one word at a time. Parents can also utilize phrase flash cards, 3 x 5 index cards on which the parents type three- or four-word phrases. The cards are flashed with the child calling out the words in each phrase as fast as possible. This type of phrase exercise is also good for training the eye to read from left to right.

Reading in Unison

Children like to read in unison, and occasionally it is desirable to have several children read at the same time. The reading material can be prepared by the parent or the teacher and given to three, four, five, or six students, who read together. This probably does not help the child very much but it should be used as a motivation factor, because reading in unison does motivate the child to read more.

Speaking and Expression

Reading aloud gives the child many opportunities to develop proper expression and voice control. It also teaches him that speaking before a group is not a terrifying experience. The parent or teacher should determine if the child is tense because of fear of the audience, and if so should try to relaxe him. The child becomes less aware of an audience if he is given exercises in the following way: (a) reading a passage into a tape recorder with no one listening, (b) reading into a microphone that is placed behind a screen, or (c) reading from a lighted area with the rest of the room darkened.

Listening to His Voice

It is important that a child be allowed to listen to a recording of his voice. A tape recorder or similar device is imperative in this matter. When a child listens to his own voice, specific faults are brought to his attention, and he is motivated to overcome them. Children like to listen to their voice, and they like other people to listen to them. By listening to their own voice, and knowing that other people will also listen, they will try to overcome their faults.

SILENT READING

An important theme of reading instruction is the mastery of silent reading. As was already stated, silent reading becomes faster than oral reading at about the third grade level. From then on, fluent and accurate silent reading is absolutely necessary for success in school, whether it is elementary school, secondary school, or college. It is also important in many of the professions. Needless to say, it opens the door to much information and pleasure.

Silent and oral reading have a great many things in common, but because one is fluent in oral reading does not mean that he will be successful in silent reading, and vice versa. The child who is painstaking and slow in oral reading and who uses his finger as a pointer, often will just skip the difficult words in silent reading that he should be solving by using word attack skills. In addition, many children who find oral reading extremely satisfying get bored when asked to read silently.

Silent reading instruction begins in the first grade just as oral reading does, but the major emphasis in the first two years of school is placed on oral reading. Both parents and teachers should know that oral and silent reading cannot be separated in the teaching process. Many young children feel very insecure in silent reading. The reason for this is that when they are reading orally they have someone listening who can not only help them pronounce the words correctly but also explain any mistakes they have made. This is not always true in silent reading, and many children feel that they make too many mistakes when no one is listening to them read. An added factor is that when a child can hear his own voice, he often feels more secure.

Reading for Information

A very important use for silent reading is obtaining information. Because children read faster silently, they can gain more information when reading this way. Children are required to read a great deal and a tremendous amount of information is covered each day; therefore, silent reading is a time-saving device. One very good exercise to determine if the child is getting information from the passage is to have him read silently and then answer several questions concerning the material he has read. If he is not reading for information at this point, he will begin to do so in order to answer these questions. A very good exercise is to have children read silently in pairs and then make up questions concerning the material to ask each other. This is not only a motivating factor, but it also helps the children gain information about each passage, because they must read it in order to devise the questions. When they have written down answers to the questions they check to see if they are right and put a grade on their papers. Another good exercise is to have children place the events in a passage in sequential order. This is not only a motivating factor but it forces the child to read for minute details; after a while the child can be timed on this, which adds not only to his speed but hopefully to his comprehension as well.

Speed Reading

It must be pointed out that speed reading should not be taught until the child has mastered oral and silent reading. When he can read silently and gain information from the material, then stand before the group and read the material orally without a flaw, the parent or teacher can begin working on speed. Concerning speed, it must be stated that speed without comprehension is not desirable. Whenever speed is increased, comprehension must remain at the 90 per cent level for the reading to be effective.

Lip Movements

Parents and teachers should observe children reading silently to determine if their lips are moving. During the first few months of the first grade, lip movements are not that important if the child is getting the meaning of the story. However, this is not true silent reading. By the end of the first grade the child should not be moving his lips when reading silently, and instruction to break this bad habit should be started.

Finger Pointing

Following the printed word with a finger is nothing to worry about in the first few months of the first grade, but it should not continue past the middle of the first grade. Instruction concerning this bad habit should also be begun early.

Parents should remember that comprehension is the most important aspect of reading. Probably the best motivation for comprehension is for the child to enjoy the story he is reading. Parents should strive to find books that their child will enjoy, and if the child reads adequately, no other motivation is necessary. Motivation will be lowered by a less interesting story or by a story that has a reading level too difficult for the child. One rule of thumb is that any material too difficult for oral reading is much too difficult for silent reading.

INDEX

A

Ability, 3
Academic life, 3
Adventure stories, 12
Alphabet, 57
Alphabet approach, 45
Alphabet books, 6
Anxiety, 53
Anxious, 53
Aphasia, 48, 85
April, 34
A reading level, 14
Arithmetic, 12
Art, 10
Auditory discrimination, 11, 34, 44, 45
Autistic children, 85

B

Babbling, 42
Baby talk, 50
Basal reader, 16, 55
Basal reader level, 58
Basal reading series, 5, 16, 27
Basic reading skills, 11
Basic sight vocabulary, 56
Bender Visual-Motor Gestalt Test, 87
Biographies, 12, 98
Biology, 91
Birth, 5, 11, 41
Birthday gift, 99
Blindness, 85
Books, 5, 96
Bookstores, 58, 94
Brain, 42
B reading level, 14

C

Capital letters, 36
Card catalog, 81
Cerebral palsy, 85
Chalkboard, 10, 11
Charts, 11
Children, 8
Children's card catalog, 81
Christmas, 99
Chronic health problems, 50
Chronological age, 44
Classrooms, 5
Classroom teacher, 8, 99
Close work, 43
College, 6, 91
Coloring books, 12
Communication, 10
Communication disorders, 85
Comprehension, 3, 4, 10, 14, 15, 16, 18, 27, 32, 55, 56, 67, 69 70
Context clues, 14, 56, 62, 63
Cooing, 42
Corrective action
  corrective activities, 66
  corrective education, 90
  corrective instruction, 32, 90
  corrective reading, 8, 17, 31, 32
  Corrective teacher, 8
Cough, 15
Crawling, 42
C reading level, 15
Creativity
  creative ability, 39
  creative reader, 97
Culturally deprived homes, 36
Curricular fields, 12
Curriculum, 10, 94

[107]

D

December, 16
Defective speech, 50
Diagnosis, 4
Dictionaries, 11, 95
Dictionary use, 65
Discrimination, 44
Discrimination clues, 65
D level, 15
Dyslexia
  dyslexic, 15, 85, 90
  dyslexic children, 88
  dyslexics, 9, 51, 87, 91, 92

E

Economic status, 39
Educational consultants, 86
Elementary class, 4
Elementary grades, 10, 68
Elementary school, 33, 83, 100
Emotional adjustment
  emotional adjustment, 53
  emotional disturbance, 50
  emotionally disturbed, 85
  emotionally maladjusted, 85
  emotional maladjustment, 49
  emotional makeup, 47
Employment, 92
Encyclopedias, 11
English, 4
Environment, 38, 93
Expression, 102, 103
Eye
  eye examination, 49
  eye movement, 45
  eyes, 10, 43
Exercises, 37

F

Factories, 6
Family, 6
Family members, 8
Favorable attitudes, 54
Fifth grade level, 51
Fifth grades, 87

Fifth reader level, 30
Finger pointing, 106
First grade, 6, 9, 35, 33
First grade basal reader, 9
First grade level, 32
First grade program, 37
First reader level, 28
Following directions, 79
Formal reading 6, 11
Formal reading instructions, 33
Formal reading program, 6
Fourth grade, 4, 7, 31, 55
Fourth grade level, 12, 16
Fourth reader level, 29
F reading level, 15
Frown, 15
Frustration, 15, 32, 53
Frustration level, 17, 18, 27, 31

G

Game board, 59
Games, 6
Geography, 4, 10, 12
Gesturing, 43
Gifted, 93
Grade level, 4, 18
Grade placement, 7, 17, 18, 27
Grades, 7
Grading system, 35
Grocery store, 10
Gross brain damage, 49
Guidance counselor, 86

H

Habits, 77
Handwriting, 10
Handwriting manual, 57
Health
  health books, 55
  health program, 9, 50
High pitched voice, 15
Historical fiction, 12
Historical materials, 74
History, 4, 10, 12, 91
Homework, 82

I

Inadequate schools, 48
Index, 80
Individual differences, 39
Individual inventory, 15
Inferior environment, 48
Inferiority, 54
Inflection, 10
Informal inventory
 informal reading inventory, 6, 7, 8, 13, 14, 32, 58
 informal reading inventory for parents, 5
 informal tests, 5
 Informal Test for Readiness, 36
Initial reading readiness, 11
Inner language, 42
Intelligence
 intellectual ability, 7
 intellectual development, 42
 intellectually normal, 9
 intelligence, low, 49
 intelligence quotient, 34, 51
Inventory, 16

J

Junior high school, 74

K

Kindergartens, 34

L

Labels, 11
Language
 language activities, 5, 38
 language art, 12
 language development, 38, 41
 language growth, 37
 language skills, 38
 language training, 37
Learning activities, 73
Learning disabilities, 85, 89, 90
Left hand, 11

Librarians, 6
Library, 10, 12, 94, 96
Lip movements, 105
Listen, 12
Listening, 4, 6, 10, 15, 43, 103
Listening language, 42
Listening skills, 3, 18, 32
Local stores, 6
Locating information, 78
Lower case letters, 36

M

Magazines, 6, 96, 98
Main idea, 78
Manuals, 10
March, 32, 34
Math, 4
Maturation, 46
Mature sentences, 38
May, 32
Mechanics, 40
Mental ability, 7, 97
Mental age, 41
Mental retardation
 mentally retarded, 15, 33
 mentally retarded child, 7, 51
 mental maturity, 44
 mental retardation, 85
Minimal brain damage, 49, 50, 51
Mixed dominance, 52
Mixed lateral dominance, 51
Modified slido-letter, 62
Multisyllable words, 11
Muscular movements, 42
Muscle control, 43
Music books, 55

N

Nature, 13
Nervousness
 nervous, 32
 nervous mannerisms, 15, 32
 nervous system, 43
Neurologically disorganized, 85
Neurologists, 86

Newspapers, 98
November, 16
Numerical grades, 7, 14
Nursery schools, 34

O

October, 16
Omit words, 15
Oral
  oral frustration level, 27
  oral language, 42, 52
  oral reading 100, 104
Organizing ideas, 79

P

Paragraph, 10, 16, 18, 78, 79
Paragraph comprehension, 69
Parks, 6
Peer acceptance, 41
Pencil, 45
Percentage points, 18
Percentages, 16
Perceptually handicapped, 86
Performance, 7
Personality maladjustment, 9
Phonic approach, 45
Phonics, 5, 56, 60
Phonics clues, 56
Phrase reading, 102
Phrasing, 68
Pictures
  picture, 6
  picture books, 12, 57
  picture cards, 6
Plants, 6
Poor teaching, 48
Prefixes, 64
Pregnancy, 89
Preprimer, 18
Preprimer level, 27
Prereading abilities, 34
Preschool activities, 65, 66
Preschooler, 38
Primer level, 28
Print, 10
Printed guides, 10

Printed page, 52
Printed words, 35
Pronounciation, 56
Psychiatrists, 86
Psychologists, 86
Psychology, 91
Puzzles, 12

R

Reader's Guide, 81
Readiness, 4, 34, 39, 56
Readiness materials, 46
Readiness program, 33
Readiness stage, 11
Reading
  reading ability, 6
  reading book, 57
  reading deficiency, 87
  reading development, 11
  reading drama, 102
  reading for information, 104
  reading in unison, 103
  reading lag, 9
  reading level, 14, 54
  reading problem, 3
  reading programs, 46
  reading progress, 75
  reading readiness, 35, 52
  reading readiness tests, 15
  reading retardation, 8, 48
  reading skills, 41, 70
Reference books, 10
Regular classroom, 5
Remedial action
  remedial activities, 8, 56, 58, 65
  remedial procedures, 88
  remedial work, 61
Report card, 77
Research, 35
Rhymes, 12
Rhythm, 12

S

School, 3
Science, 13
Science books, 55

Scissors, 45
School age population, 48
Scientific material, 72
Second grade level, 101
Second reader level, 28
Self esteem, 41
Self image, 44
Sensory growth, 43
September, 16, 32, 34
Sequential unfolding, 41
Short story, 18
Sight vocabulary, 56, 58
Silent reading, 50, 104
Similariies, 44
Sixth grade, 18
Sixth grade level, 7, 31
Skills, 6, 10
Skimming, 80
Slido-letter, 61, 62
Slow learner, 85
Small groups, 79
Social adjustment, 53
Social control, 43
Social studies, 4, 10, 12
Socioeconomic status, 38
Speak, 12
Speaking, 10, 103
Speaking abilities, 6
Special clinics, 8
Speech
  speech habits, 43, 50
  speech therapists, 86
Speed, 10
Speed reading, 105
Spelling, 4, 12, 88
Spoken language, 42
Squint, 15
Story books, 6
Structural analysis, 64
Study skills, 77, 84
Substitute words, 15
Suffixes, 64
Symbol blindness, 9
Symbols, 33, 40

T

Talking, 46
Teaching
teachable time, 41
teacher, 5, 6, 75
teacher-prepared materials, 11
teacher's manual, 5
Television, 58
Tension, 15
Testing session, 32
Textbooks, 10
Thinking, 43
Third grade, 16, 18
Third grade level, 16
Third reader level, 29
Tonal inflections, 42
Tools
  tool, 11, 12
  tool subject, 13
Travel books, 12

U

Unorthodox way, 39
Unreadiness, 39

V

Vision problem, 9
Visual, 34
Visual discrimination, 44, 88
Vocabulary, 11, 43, 57, 58, 63

W

Walking, 42, 46
Wechsler Intelligence Scale for
  Children, 87
Wiggle, 15
Word
  word attack, 32
  word attack skills, 3
  word blindness, 51
  word calling, 10
  word lists, 18, 58
  word recognition, 3, 15, 16, 32,
    55, 56, 63
  word recognition skills, 4
  Word Recognition Test, 16, 20, 21,
    22, 23, 24, 25, 26
Write, 12
Writing, 10, 12, 43

Y

Yawn, 15
Young child, 6

Z

Zoos, 6